RAISING CONFIDENT BLACK KIDS

RAISING CONFIDENT BLACK KIDS

A Comprehensive Guide for Empowering Parents and Teachers of Black Children

M.J. Fievre

Mango Publishing

CORAL GABLES

For permission requests, please contact the publisher at:
Mango Publishing Group
2850 S Douglas Road, 2nd Floor
Coral Gables, FL 33134 USA
info@mango.bz

For special orders, quantity sales, course adoptions and corporate sales, please email the publisher at sales@mango.bz. For trade and wholesale sales, please contact Ingram Publisher Services at customer.service@ingramcontent.com or +1.800.509.4887.

Raising Confident Black Kids: A Comprehensive Guide for Empowering Parents and Teachers of Black Children

Library of Congress Cataloging-in-Publication number: LCCN has been requested
ISBN: (print) 978-1-64250-558-0, (ebook) 978-1-64250-559-7
BISAC category code EDU038000, EDUCATION / Student Life & Student Affairs

Printed in the United States of America

To my goddaughter Imane.

As I wrote this book, you were never far from my thoughts.

Table of Contents

Overview

Introduction

In the introduction, I explain why I decided to write this book, who I am, and what you can expect to find in the pages of *Raising Confident Black Kids*. Also discussed is who this book is intended for, and how reading it can help many people who are either raising Black children or have Black children in their lives.

Chapter 1: "The Talk"

"The Talk" is about the essential series of conversations that all parents of Black children must have with their kids to ensure their safety and give them a basic understanding of systemic racism. Included in this chapter are: topics for discussing race with your kids, an explanation of how having regular discussions about racism with Black children will help ensure their safety and make them stronger anti-racists, and an explanation of how kids learn about racism without any intervention from adults.

Chapter 2: How to Talk to Your Baby or Toddler about Race

This chapter explains how to start talking to your Black children about race and racism, starting in infancy through age three. It is written in an easy-to-read format that explains what your child understands and observes about race on their own and provides age-appropriate guidelines for discussing racism with Black children as well as suggestions for ensuring they grow in a diverse environment.

Chapter 3: How to Talk to Young Children about Race

This chapter explains how to discuss race with your pre-k and elementary school-aged children (ages three to eleven). There is a discussion of the kinds of racist incidents children this age face, and suggestions for activities you can do with your child during this stage of development that will help them understand systemic racism while fostering a healthy self-image. It also explains the serious impact of racism on young children.

Chapter 4: How to Talk to Your Tweens and Teens about Race

This chapter suggests ways of discussing racism with Black tweens and teens (ages eleven and up) and how to reach out to them about a very difficult topic. Included in the chapter are answers to questions like: What do I do if my child says something racist, or displays behaviors that reflect ingrained colorism? There are anecdotes about the kind of racism kids this age face, some personal stories, and

suggestions for activities your child can do to help them feel confident
and empowered as they mature into independence.

Chapter 5: Activism and Allyship

This chapter explains safe ways to engage your child in anti-racist
and other forms of activism, and profiles some young people who
are engaging in the activist movement. It explains what qualities to
look for in an ally and what performative allyship is, and tells the
story of a writer who was exploited by performative allies during the
publication of a book she coauthored with a white writer.

Chapter 6: Racial Profiling
and Police Encounters

This article explores racial profiling, not only by police, but by the
general public, and the impact that has on Black citizens. It explains
the different types of police encounters and what your rights are
in each of these situations. It discusses what happens when police
encounters turn deadly and how to stay safe. There is an age-by-
age guide to talking to your children about the police, and further
information about the problems people with mental illness and/or
disabilities face when dealing with police.

Chapter 7: How to Explain
Systemic Racism to Your Child

This chapter discusses the overarching systemic racism in the United
States and looks closely at statistical data that proves there is a

disparity between whites and Blacks in America in terms of income equality, the criminal justice system, and healthcare. This chapter explains how to fight systemic racism and offers tips on dealing with racists.

Intermission: Shocking Racist Traditions

This section explores the hidden, often unwritten history of racism through artifacts, songs, advertising and other memorabilia. It discusses the movement to remove monuments that glorify a racist and imperialist past and offers suggestions on how to introduce your children to the kind of history they won't read about in their school textbooks.

Chapter 8: Microaggressions, "Reverse Racism," and Intersectionality

In this chapter, you'll learn to recognize (and disarm) microaggressions and overt acts of racism. We'll discuss commonly used phrases that are actually racist, and ways to respond to non-Black friends who say racist things. Also explored is intersectionality, what it is, and why it's important to understand.

Chapter 9: How to Encourage Creativity and Build Self-Confidence in Your Child

This chapter is an age-by-age guide to building confidence and self-esteem in your Black child. There are suggested activities for nurturing creativity in your child (broken down by age), and

suggestions on how to develop an appreciation for Black arts
and culture.

Chapter 10: How to Teach your Child to Self-Advocate

This chapter explains how to raise a Black child who knows how to
self-advocate and why this is an important skill for them to develop.
It explores racism in the school system and shows you how to identify
anti-racist teachers. It discusses the physical and mental toll of
racism on Black children and offers coping mechanisms to help ease
the stress and damage caused by racial trauma. It also discusses the
burdens Black parents face when parenting their kids. We look at the
spike in Black suicides and offer suggestions on how you can help
your child through difficult times.

Chapter 11: How to Make Your Community a Safer One

This chapter suggests ways to involve your neighbors, and what
you can do to make your home and community safer; it includes a
resource guide of different tools to help you in your efforts. It also
looks at the complex problem of informal segregation in the United
States and the issue of gentrification.

Chapter 12: When You're a Non-Black Parent to your Black Child

This chapter was written especially for non-Black parents of mixed-race and Black children. We'll discuss transracial adoption and the backlash families often face when adopting a child outside of their race. Also offered are tips for dealing with extended family members and other people who may have racist tendencies. We'll discuss what your Black child needs from you in terms of support and cultural nurturing and whether transracial adoptions harm Black culture. Also explained are some of the unique challenges your Black or mixed-race child may face growing up with a non-Black parent.

Conclusion & Acknowledgments

Introduction

In January of 2020, I published my book *Badass Black Girl*, an empowerment guide for young Black girls. I wrote the book because I wanted Black girls to receive the kind of advice I didn't get growing up in Haiti. I wanted my readers to grow into powerful Black women who understand that, although the odds of succeeding in life are stacked against them, they can prevail against those odds. Almost immediately, I began to see the difference my book was making in the lives of young Black women, and I was proud of the work I had done to raise their self-esteem and offer them a path toward promising futures. But then, the media began reporting on the kind of news stories that have been prevalent for eons, stories of Black men and women who had been killed for inexplicable reasons. I began following these stories, and the testimony of pain shared by the parents and families of Black people who were killed in the course of a typical day.

On February 23, Ahmaud Arbery was followed by three white men while out for a run. The men chased him in a truck and shot him down in the middle of the street. Investigators have reported that one of the men used a racial slur as Mr. Arbery lay on the street dying. In the wake of his assassination, Arbery's mother, Wanda Cooper-Jones, poignantly stated in an interview, "I had to explain to Ahmaud that he would sometimes be disliked because of the color of his skin, but when he left our home to go for a jog, I never thought I needed to be worried. Ahmaud wasn't killed because he was doing a crime, so why would he have been targeted if it wasn't just for hate?"[1]

Shortly after midnight on March 13, a team of Louisville, KY policemen, executing a no-knock warrant, used a battering ram to break down the door of twenty-six-year-old Breonna Taylor's apartment. After a brief confrontation, the police opened fire. Ms. Taylor died after she was shot at least eight times. In the aftermath of her killing, Taylor's mother, Tamika Palmer, told the *Courier Journal,* "She had a whole plan on becoming a nurse and buying a house and then starting a family. Breonna had her head on straight, and she was a very decent person. She didn't deserve this. She wasn't that type of person."[2] Ms. Taylor, a paramedic, had no prior criminal history.

By the beginning of June 2020, hundreds of thousands of protestors had taken to the streets to protest in the aftermath of George Floyd's death. Curfews were enforced, the National Guard was called out, and I watched as American streets were rendered hazy in clouds of tear gas and mace. Floyd had been held down by Minneapolis police, one of whom knelt on his neck for an excruciating eight minutes, forty-six seconds while he cried out that he couldn't breathe, and made a plaintive call, "Mama, Mama…" for his deceased mother.[3]

Their names, Ahmaud Arbery, Breonna Taylor, and George Floyd, were the tail end of a litany of names I had been hearing for years, and I added them to the list that was growing in my mind along with Michael Brown, Eric Garner, Trayvon Martin, and many others, a list that could fill volumes of books with names of those who had been killed far too young for no good reason. I was filled with mixed emotions: anger, grief, despondency, a sense of panic and fear at the

---

1   Cooper-Jones (2020)
2   Costello (2020)
3   Fernandez and Burch (2020)

continuing violence, and hopelessness at the understanding there was little I could do to make a difference.

I knew instinctively that the people behind these names had all had some version of "the Talk" growing up, and that, despite the best efforts of their parents, they too had all died in modern lynchings simply because they were in the wrong place at the wrong time. I call these deaths "modern lynchings" because, too often, there is a lack of justice despite the preponderance of evidence showing that systemic racism is still killing our people in violent, senseless ways. The sad truth is that parents of Black kids can only do so much to make sure their kids survive racism, but key to that understanding is that **there IS so much you can do** as a parent to make sure your kids understand what they need to do to thrive. Having "the Talk" is a mandatory part of raising a Black child.

Some parents believe that they are protecting their children by avoiding any discussion of racism and want above all to preserve their children's innocence. No one wants their kid to feel like they are different or unappreciated. But any Black child who is unprepared to deal with a racist culture is growing up unprotected in a dangerous environment. Sooner or later, every Black child learns about racism; the question is whether they are going to learn about it from you, their parents, or by experiencing it firsthand with no preparation for the smack of its impact.

I had been planning to write about "the Talk" even before the latest media reports came out. As a K–12 teacher in South Florida, I have had plenty of uncomfortable conversations with my students (and their parents) about race. In 2012, the death of Trayvon Martin was disturbing for many of my students whose experiences are shaped by being Black; if their teacher was not attuned to the part of their being that is race, then it could be very difficult to understand and respond to their humanity.

I'd spent so much time building my students up, helping them feel comfortable in their skin, and affirming their identities. Teachers are by nature creators of safe spaces, and initiators of difficult conversations. But like so many teachers, I was struggling to find the words to explain why Black people are treated differently, and why what happened to Trayvon Martin was not an isolated incident of racism in America.

These conversations led me to look more closely at how we can teach our Black kids to stay safe, while simultaneously protecting and building their self-esteem. I began to research the issue and speak to school counselors and psychologists to find strategies parents and teachers can use with their children to broach an uncomfortable but necessary topic.

Talking to Black kids about racism is different than the conversations non-Black parents have with their white kids. Non-Black families who choose to be anti-racist have the privilege of initiating the conversation from a removed distance where the goal is more centered around teaching kids how to be an effective ally to Black people.[4] For parents of Black children, the conversation is one that has been handed down for centuries and is centered on teaching children to mitigate danger through a series of "don'ts" that can sometimes be contradictory and confusing.

- Don't go into "that" neighborhood.
- Don't sass white people, especially white men.
- Don't reach into your pocket for your license if you are pulled over by the police.
- Don't resist arrest.
- Don't be confrontational with white men, especially white policemen.

---

4 McDonald (2020)

- Don't play loud music in your car.

- Don't stay out late.

- Don't leave home without your ID.

- Don't touch anything in the store if you aren't going to purchase it.

- Don't leave a store without having a bag for your purchase and a receipt.

- Don't go out in a crowd.

- Don't go out alone.

- Don't loiter.

- Don't run.

- Don't walk too slowly.

- And so forth...

While the United States was experiencing protests in early June 2020, a Houston teenager named Cameron Welch posted a Tik Tok video that went viral; it showed him repeating the "don'ts" he'd learned from his mother.[5] A series of other videos took social media by storm, showing other parents having these same discussions with their kids. Suddenly "the Talk" was all over the news.

Why were people reacting so strongly to these videos? Because they brought the implications of parenting Black kids into the spotlight, and showed some of the challenges all parents of Black children face, challenges I knew I wanted to address in my writing, in the hopes that parents could have a toolkit to help nurture their children and offer them a little more security and understanding of how to keep their kids safe. Against this backdrop, I began writing.

------

5   Welch (2020)

Who is this book for?

Raising Confident and Empowered Black Kids includes everything Black and multiracial families need to know to raise empowered, confident children. From the realities of living while Black to age-appropriate ways to discuss racism with your child, I provide a much-needed resource for parents of Black kids everywhere.

It's hard to balance protecting your child's innocence with preparing them for the realities of Black life. When—and how—do you approach racism with your children? How do you protect their physical and mental health while also preparing them for a country (a world!) full of systemic racism? Now, there's a guide to help you teach your kids how to thrive, even when it feels like the world is against them. From racial profiling and police encounters to the whitewashed lessons of history taught in schools, raising Black kids is no easy feat. I pass on the tips and guidance that have helped me educate my Black students, including ways to:

- encourage creativity and build self-confidence in your kid

- engage in activism and help build a safer community with and for your child

- explain systemic racism, intersectionality, and microaggressions

This book is intended for anyone parenting a Black child, whether or not you yourself are Black. The family dynamics in the United States have shifted enough that, quite often, Black children are being raised in mixed-race families. I've included a chapter for non-Black parents of Black and mixed-race children, and I've shared some of my personal experiences with Afro-Latinx and Caribbean parents of Black kids.

The book, which puts current events in the context of history, the Civil Rights movement, and the ongoing fight for equity, can also be useful to allies of Black children who need a resource that helps them understand the challenge of raising a confident, empowered Black child in a racist culture.

Raising Confident Black Kids is also for teachers and counselors who encourage their students to choose action over silence. Racism has created an underlying tension in which many Black students feel invisible in a school system they feel does not do enough to support them and their community. I know many educators want specific changes, including legislative actions to dismantle long-standing systemic inequities such as the school-to-prison pipeline and the inequitable way that schools are funded. May this book become an important tool as educators and school leaders continue to listen and commit to the hard and necessary practice of anti-racist work.

Whoever you are, dear reader, I want to encourage you not to shy away from tough conversations about race or any kind of injustice or inequity. Hopefully, my work will teach you how you can help your children turn their complicated feelings and thoughts into meaningful action, how to help them raise their voices—because these Black voices are so powerful.

M.J. Fievre
BadassBlackGirl.com

Chapter 1

"The Talk"

"The Talk": An Unavoidable Conversation

Talking about race with any child can be a sticky, complicated, and uncomfortable process, but it's a necessary part of raising a child who has a clear understanding of the world around them. Talking to Black kids about race is not only important, it can be a life-or-death series of conversations. Black people, and overwhelmingly Black boys and young men, are statistically more likely to become homicide victims, are more likely to be arrested, and are more subject to dying during the course of a police encounter than any other race.[6] Having these conversations isn't a one-and-done deal. Rather, it's a process. Raising a Black child will require you to be prepared for an ongoing discussion about race and systemic racism, and how to dismantle oppressive societal constructs.

If that sounds complicated, it is, but don't worry. Start simple and start early. As your child grows, the conversations will take on more complexity and depth. You may be asking yourself, "Why do I need to talk about racism with my three-year-old? The child is still learning to use the potty." Or, "How do I get past the discomfort of explaining racism to my kid?" Or, "How much does my child really think about

---

race?" There are dozens of questions all parents of Black children have when they think about explaining racism to their kids.[7] We'll look at some of these questions and others.

Keep in mind:

You don't really have much of a choice about whether you'll have "the Talk."

It's more a matter of where and when. The realities of racism are all over the news and on social media, and if you haven't had a conversation with your child about race, sooner or later, chances are, your child will ask questions about racism. "Kids are learning and hearing about race regardless of whether parents are talking to them about it," says Dr. Margaret Hagerman, a sociologist and author of *White Kids: Growing Up with Privilege in a Racially Divided America.*[8] As your child grows, the possibility of having a racist encounter increases, and so do the stakes of the conversations. Your child's safety depends on these discussions. But even before they reach the age of maturity, Black kids may start to feel they are somehow "less than" their non-Black playmates. Even very small children may find they are left out of playground games because of the color of their skin. They may find there is no representation of Black characters in the television programs they watch, or when there are Black characters, those characters are often stereotyped or problematic. It's harder to find Black dolls and other toys on store shelves, and Black dolls are often presented with white features or hair that doesn't match the natural texture of Black hair. It can be frustrating.

Many Afro-Caribbean and Afro-Latino parents don't think of themselves (or their children) as Black, and because of that my

---

7 Paschall-Brown (2020)

8 Timmis (2019)

Dominican friend Katherine confessed to me that this chapter was really triggering to her. "Oh, no!" she realized, "I *am* raising a Black child!" Your child's Caribbean ties or their Latinidad will not save them from racism, because racism doesn't differentiate between "levels" of Blackness. Despite your ethnic identification or the language you may speak, Afro-Caribbean and Afro-Latinos are first seen as Black to white America. Having "the Talk" will require some deep introspection if you're like Katherine. You will have to acknowledge your internalized racism, the painful legacy left by generations of Caribbean and Latinx people who were taught about the superiority of Eurocentricity and whiteness, and recognize the ways you perpetuate and uphold white supremacy. Know that your oppression is bound up and intertwined with the oppression of the African American community. We are one Black people.

If you want examples of questionable engrained concepts of Blackness and racism in Latinx communities, think of the controversial show *Siempre Bruja* on Netflix, which stereotypically portrays the main character, a Black woman named Carmen Eguiluz, as a slave/witch who is in love with a white Hispanic plantation owner, the man who owns her—quite a disturbing trope. In Miami, blackface has been used to mock Black characters in Spanish-language TV and theater (Google "Three Windows on a Cruise") with little dispute, and the *Miami Herald* recently came under fire for including an insert filled with racist (in this case, anti-Semitic) creeds.

Your heart will get broken—very often.

Young kids have no filters on what they say, and where they say the things they say, and they will ask you questions that will break your heart. You can teach them what is and is not appropriate to talk about in public, but be prepared to answer some tough questions at home. Questions like: "Why do they hate me for something that's not my fault?" or "Why do the police want to kill me?" Stay supportive in your responses even when the conversations are deeply disturbing and troubling.

CNN and Sesame Street partnered to create a town hall on racism, which aims to help young kids learn how to stand up to racism; it is available online. Raising Race-Conscious Children (www. raceconscious.org) has curated a list of "100 Race-Conscious Things You Can Say to Your Child to Advance Racial Justice," and the quotes on the website model language that has actually been used in a conversation with a child regarding race (and other identity-markers such as gender and class); it's an excellent resource for parents who want to get the conversation started. Embrace Race (www.embracerace.org) also has a series of webinars and action guides for talking to kids about race, and The Conscious Kid (www. theconsciouskid.org) offers kids' books, interviews, and other critical conversation-starters.

It gets easier.

Learn to live with the discomfort you're feeling, and how to corral that energy in a positive direction. Teach your kids how to do the same. Teach them they can talk to you about anything. We'll look more closely at how to handle some of the more day-to-day problems your kids might face further in the book, and how to address these with constructive conversations.

Don't give up.

Black kids need help developing self-esteem. As a parent, you'll want to raise a child who feels confident and secure with who they want to be, despite other people's racist attitudes. It will require a lot of work on your part to counter the negative messages they may be receiving from people around them. Remind them that it's "not about you," and encourage them to forge their identity as an individual as much as you can.

Check yourself!

Pay attention to how you talk about other races in front of your kids. If you laugh at racially insensitive jokes or mock other people's accents, knock it off. Kids are sensitive to bias, and they depend on you to model proper behavior. I grew up in an Afro-Caribbean community where calling someone "African" was considered the ultimate insult, and grown-ups thought it was okay to make fun of the "chintok." On many occasions, I've been told, "You're pretty for a Black girl"—and often it came from Afro-Latinx people.

We MUST do better.

Parents sometimes express understandable trepidation at the thought of initiating talks about race because of the impulse to protect their child's innocence. However, a study from *Developmental Science* has shown that that children as young as three months old are already beginning to make distinctions about race, physical differences, and cultural differences and show preference for faces of their own race.[9] Racial stereotyping begins very early. By the time a child reaches toddler age, they are noticing race and drawing conclusions, based in part on cues they receive from their parents' body language and level of tension. They look to you for approval in a variety of ways, including who they have interactions with during playtime—and if your reactions are affected by the race of other people, they notice that too.

But racism is something that can be internalized by about the ages of two to four without any input from you, based solely on how prevalent it is in society, so it's important that you remain vigilant and prepared to counter the messages your kids are receiving from around them every day.

---

9   Kelly et al. (2005)

By the age of twelve, some children have already developed long-standing prejudices about racial groups.

It's more complicated than just development. Your kids also have to deal with other people's bias toward them based on skin color. By four years old, Black preschoolers are already seen as more "problematic" based on data about expulsions from preschools.[10] They also have to deal with "adultification," which is the likelihood Black children will be perceived as more mature or older than they are, based solely on their race.[11] In girls, this begins to happen at about the age of five, and with boys, by the age of ten.

Talking to your children about racism will:

- prepare them for racist encounters and arm them with the tools they will need to survive and thrive in the face of racism
- allow you to have a continuing dialogue about race sparked by current events
- teach them to understand their civil rights and how to exercise them

It's okay to let kids know that you don't think systemic racism is fair, and that you wish you didn't have to have "the Talk" with them. Let them know you'd rather not, but that you love them and want to teach them how to stay safe in the face of adversity. Remember to provide them with specific guidelines about their rights and the methods of exercising those rights that they'll need to understand to keep themselves safe. (We'll go over some basic civil rights in a subsequent chapter, but I encourage you to look into Colin Kaepernik's "Know Your Rights" campaign as well.)

---

10   Anderson (2015)
11   Lopez (2016)

Along with the "don'ts" you may find yourself teaching your children, you may want to teach them some "dos." Having positive instructions will counter some of the negative but necessary lessons you have to teach your kids.

- Do know your rights and how to exercise them effectively.

- Do remain calm.

- Do ask questions.

- Do be proud of who you are.

- Do treat everyone with respect.

- And so forth…

The questions your kids ask will tend to be about three areas:

Personal Identity

No one wants to be known simply as "the Black kid" and your child may find they are frustrated with being pigeon-holed into an identity they had no part in creating. It's important to affirm that identity is much more complicated than just race, and that despite other people's attempts to put them into one designation, their individuality matters in addition to their race. You'll want your kid to be proud of being Black, but let them know that people can and will learn to appreciate them for the traits that make them unique, like how kind they are to other people, or how talented they are in areas that are difficult for others to excel at. One of my Black students could solve a Rubik's cube in less than twenty minutes without having watched the YouTube videos, and another was a self-taught throat singer. At ten, my goddaughter Imane is already a gifted chef, but what really makes her unique is how valued she makes the people around her feel: she sees (really *sees*) other people. My teenage nephew Marc-Olivier excels at tennis, and he's also very apt when it comes to reading a room and solving a problem.

Racism and White Privilege

The questions your kids ask in these areas will tend to be "whys" and those can be some of the most difficult questions to answer. For example, "Why don't the white kids play with me?" "Why is it that Black people are more likely to go to prison?" "Why is Sophie always the teacher's favorite?" Some of these will leave you scratching your head for answers, and it can become frustrating to explain the reasons for white privilege or racist sentiments to your children, but take a deep breath, think about your answers, and proceed patiently. You can define white privilege as an unspoken advantage that white people have based on the color of their skin. For children, you can explain to them that being white is like receiving an extra handful of candy on Halloween before they even leave the house to go trick or treating, or that it's like receiving extra credit on a school assignment just for writing their name on the page.

Your child's questions will be made complicated by certain family dynamics. Black children who are part of a transracial or mixed family might struggle to understand the "rules" associated with race (and I elaborate on that in a later chapter). In the case of Afro-Caribbean and Afro-Latinx families, anti-Blackness has deep and complicated roots in the community, where fair-skinned people are frequently viewed as the ideal and receive better treatment, and assimilation is presented as the path to equality.

Other Non-White Minority Groups

As they grow, your child will begin to notice other non-white minorities and the challenges they face. For example, right now, the United States is detaining many South and Central American and Mexican refugees at immigration detention facilities. Your kid may want to know why these people are being detained, or why the US is so eager to deport people from these countries. Try to understand that these questions are an opportunity to widen your child's understanding of the world, and the politics of other countries. Encourage them to find their own answers by researching what problems people in other places face in their home countries, but also broaden their understanding of other groups by taking them to events that celebrate heritage and can educate them about customs and culture.

When you arm your child with positive steps toward combating racism, you teach them that they have the power to make a difference. They may not always have the opportunity to make a difference against another person's hard lined racist notions, but they can at least be in control of how they react to the situation.

Haitian American writer Fabienne Josaphat's story about a racist encounter shows the limitations Black parents face when discussing race with people in the community.

I'm sad. America makes me sad. A story:

Someone left a bike behind my house, out on the main road, but right behind an oak tree. It's a used bike, but in decent condition, I guess, and the way it's stationed, it looks like it might belong to us. I can tell because everyone who walks by or bikes past it looks at our house, wondering, "Why did they park this bike here?"

It's been there three days now, and it's become clear the bike is abandoned. Of course, it means in my mind, someone might have stolen it and ditched it, or that it gave out and they couldn't ride it home. Either way, no one came to claim it.

Gordon's (my husband's) first instinct is that it was probably stolen, and he wants to call the cops. I say NO. I prefer to find an alternative. I don't like the police's presence. And I don't want to call attention to us, since we are one of the few Black families in this subdivision. It's the reality I live in. So we're discussing: Pull it out of the bushes? Put it out somewhere visible? Put out a call on the neighborly app?

Gordon goes on the neighbor network app. Is anyone missing a bike? There is one behind our house. Immediately, this man responds. He thinks it's his. In five minutes, he shows up and I meet him out back.

It's not his bike; his was stolen and it's a beach cruiser. And then, here is where the story saddens me.

"I feel bad," he says. "I have the crime on video, it wasn't very clear, maybe a little grainy, but I know it was three kids, two white kids and one Black, and they took my bike, and I think I saw the Black kid here."

Me: "Here, as in this community?"

Him: "Yes, you know, I saw him sitting out, playing basketball. So I felt horrible, you know how moms are, but I went over there, and I feel bad for accusing him of stealing my bike."

I want to burst into tears. Yes. He's white. Yes, I know what it's like for moms. I know what it's like for Black moms, and you're speaking to me and I'm obviously Black. You accused a random Black kid of stealing your bike without knowing for sure whether it was him or not, just because your grainy video told you it was a Black boy. Right now, in America, a Black mother is consoling her son and discussing at dinner why he got accused, and why it will always be that way. Must it always be that way? I'm so sad, and so angry.

(Fabienne Josaphat)

The hardest part of having "the Talk" may be knowing that no matter what you tell your child, or how well you prepare them to face the world when you're not with them, it might not be enough to change the outcome of a racist altercation. Have "the Talk" anyway. It will enable them to at least understand what they can change and what they cannot change.

Silence Is Not an Option

As the parent of a Black child, you'll find that you're nurturing the development of some basic but important concerns that come easier for other parents. These include developing pride and an understanding of racial and/or cultural heritage, an understanding of other racial/cultural groups, and an understanding of how racism works and the best methods to disarm a racist incident or remain safe during a racist encounter.

It can feel like a heavy responsibility, but it's necessary.

Not saying anything is much worse than feeling awkward. While you may find yourself stumbling for answers or feeling awkward about responding to questions, ignoring racism won't make it go away, and your child will appreciate your candor. It's okay to say, "I don't know an easy way to say this." Go ahead and acknowledge your discomfort. It will teach your child that you are willing to fight past the discomfort of the topic to make sure they understand what you want them to know. It's okay to admit you either don't know or don't understand all the nuances behind racism. Not knowing isn't an obstacle. It's an opportunity to figure things out together with your kids, and it shows them that you are willing to listen to their concerns seriously and find solutions that work.

Not discussing racism with your child when they try to initiate a discussion with you sends a clear message to them that their feelings aren't understood and respected, and that can shut down conversations about other things troubling them. It's better to foster an open channel of communication with your kids about even the most difficult subjects. If you are completely honest with your kids, it sends the message to them that you care and respect them, and this can help you foster a long-lasting, nurturing relationship that endures into their adulthood.[12] Your kid looks to you to help them develop an understanding of how society works, and they need your help navigating the world around them. Otherwise they can become overwhelmed and confused by how scary and pervasive these problems seem to be.

_____

12   Holohan (2020)

Your kids won't know as much about the issue at first as you do. You don't need to sit down and have a long talk with your three-year-old about civil rights or microaggression or anything that's terribly complicated. You can approach the topic in an age-appropriate manner that sets the stage for later conversations that go more in-depth into the issues of racism. We'll discuss how to approach the topic a little later in this book with an age-by-age guide.

Storytelling can really help you engage your child in meaningful conversation.[13] For small children, for example, *Chrysanthemum* by Kevin Henkes is a story about a little mouse who thinks her name is marvelous, until she starts school. On her first day of school, the children tease her because her name is the longest name in the class. However, after some kind and insightful words from a music teacher, the other children in Chrysanthemum's class realize that having a name like Chrysanthemum is quite special and unique. The Race Project (www.understandingrace.org) developed discussion questions and other activities that allow parents to use stories like *Chrysanthemum* to discuss race and racism with their children, and celebrate individuality and ancestry. Children then learn that individual differences among people are positive and to be appreciated and celebrated, not criticized. They learn that the racism directed at them is not a reflection of their value as individuals.

If you are a Black parent, there's a good chance you are also trying to process your own ongoing experiences with racism or racist incidents in the news. Your kids may see you upset or angry and not understand why. Explaining to them what you are feeling, and why, teaches them how to deal with their own, often overwhelming, emotions. You can approach these discussions in an age-appropriate manner: "Mommy is sad because I saw something on television that I don't think was nice." If you have an older Black child, chances are

---

13   Grose (2020)

they have access to the internet and may run into information or videos of racist incidents on their own, and these can be particularly troubling to a young person who has not had "the Talk" yet. If you can initiate a discussion now, before they find information on their own, they'll at least have begun to understand the harsh reality, and won't be forced to draw (sometimes unreliable) conclusions on their own.

Children begin to notice race distinctions a lot earlier than many of us realize, and it's easy for them to internalize these, in part, because they often have no outlet to discuss what they are seeing and experiencing with an adult. Ask questions and be prepared to have some long talks about what your kids are seeing and/or experiencing, and how you have dealt with the same kinds of experiences. This will show them that they are not alone, and that you understand and love them.

I recently shared this story with one of my nieces:

Growing up in Haiti, I did not get the race talk.[14] My first face-to-face experience with racism happened after migrating to Miami. My first year of college, I biked to school. A car once slowed down next to me, so a young white man could throw a cup full of milkshake at my chest, calling me the N-word, while the other two laughed. That was my first week in America, and an accelerated lesson in racism. It happened many other times—the N-word call, I mean. In front of the bowling alley as I waited for my sorority sister to pick me up. On my way to a Chinese restaurant for lunch during a summer writing workshop at the University of Miami. There's not one day when I don't consciously think: "I am female. I am Black." It guides my decisions every day. If you never have to think about the space you occupy in a room, on a sidewalk, in front of a bowling alley, you're privileged.

---

14   Ziyad (2019)

Once you start having "the Talk" with your own kid, a lot of the worries you have will ease up, though they may never completely go away. At the very least you'll know your child has some of the tools they need to be strong, independent, and successful in navigating toward a bright future. In the next chapters, we'll go over some age-appropriate discussion and activity prompts for kids of all ages, but for right now, know that by thinking and reading about "the Talk," you've taken the first step toward building a strong, open relationship with a child who can look to you for guidance. You CAN do this. You've already started!

Chapter 2

How to Talk to Your Baby or Toddler about Race

Why on Earth would anyone talk to an infant or toddler (ages zero to three) about racism? At six months of age, they can barely figure out how to get their fist out of their mouth, let alone understand the overarching system of oppression that has been a hallmark of world governments for centuries. Besides, you feel lucky if they give you a "Mama" at that age.

The truth is that your innocent little knuckle sucker is already noticing things like skin tone,[15] and it's your job to guide them to an understanding of racism and how it will impact them over the course of their lives. It's not an easy or fun prospect, but it's crucial if you want to raise a child who feels empowered to make a difference in the world, or even just has an understanding that the issue has nothing to do with them personally.

And if kids start developing biases at an early age, it's also important to note that they start experiencing the brunt of racism very early as well. Talking to children about racism is not a simple process. You'll want to keep their developmental level in mind, so that you know

---

15 "An age-by-age guide to talking to your kids about racism" (n.d.)

they understand what exactly it is you are talking to them about and what they may be experiencing.

Infants and Toddlers

Only one-third of the births in the United States are Black babies, and yet the infant mortality rate places Black babies in a position where they make up three fourths of the deaths. Black mothers are three to four times more likely than white non-Hispanic women to die during pregnancy and childbirth.[16] The discrepancy is due to several factors, including that doctors are less likely to respond to a Black woman's health concerns. Even high-profile Black women are not immune to medical neglect. Tennis star Serena Williams experienced complications that led to blood clots in her lungs after the caesarean birth of her daughter, and her doctors failed to heed her advice to put her on blood thinners although she explained having a blood clotting condition.[17]

These kinds of concerns led Christian Farmer of Cleveland, Ohio, to set up the nonprofit Birthing Beautiful Communities to provide Black doulas to pregnant women and postpartum support so that they would have a culturally sensitive advocate with them during the labor and delivery process and in the first year of their child's life, which is a crucial time for a Black infant.[18]

Black mothers are more likely to be tested for prenatal drug abuse, and in some cases, even if they test negative for drugs, they are treated as though they are responsible for things like low birth weight. This can lead to separation of mother and infant by Child Protective Services, which can impact the crucial bonding period right after a

---

16   Edwards-Luce (2020)
17   Salam (2018)
18   Lakhani (2019)

baby is born. Having a Black doula as an advocate may decrease the chances that a Black woman will run into complications during her pregnancy or right after birth.

How to Talk with Your Child about Race During This Stage

Read books and watch videos that celebrate diversity

Through much of this stage, your child will communicate through "wants" and "needs." Even if they are nonverbal, reading to kids at this age and watching educational shows like *Sesame Street* helps them develop language skills. Find age-appropriate books and videos for them to read or watch with you that have a cast of characters that is diverse, positive, and doesn't rely on stereotypes. One of my favorite Afro-Caribbean writers has authored wonderful picture books with diverse characters: Make sure to check out Edwidge Danticat's *My Mommy Medicine* and *Mama's Nightingale.*

As your child is exploring, take that opportunity to start teaching them that differences are normal, and point out similarities in their environment. You can hold your skin up to theirs and show them, "Look, Daddy's skin is brown like yours. Mommy's skin is different." Or, for example, "Look, that little boy has red hair." Kids at this age are starting to learn colors. Show them the world is made of rainbows.

PBS Kids has published a list of books to read together as a family, to encourage conversations about race and diversity with children. The titles include *Sulwe* by Lupita Nyong'o (author) and Vashti Harrison (illustrator), *Whose Knees are These?* by Jabari Asim (author) and LeUyen Pham (illustrator), and *Hair Love* by Matthew A. Cherry (author) and Vashti Harrison (illustrator), among many other treasures.

Normalize and celebrate differences every day

Infants and toddlers learn from repetition and observation. At this age, you can begin teaching kids that differences in skin tone, and other differences like disabilities and different sizes, are normal. Even if it's unlikely that your child is understanding everything you say to them, you can practice acknowledging the differences so that your child grows to see people as unique and equal. Stay positive about the differences your toddler sees. If your child points out a difference in someone's skin tone, tell them how wonderful you think it is that people come in a variety of shades. As they grow older, it'll be easier for them to recognize instances of microaggression and racism directed at them, if they've learned to acknowledge and celebrate differences.

Avoid "color-blindness"

Yes, even Black parents are guilty of this: "I don't see color," they say, wishing the world could be so simple. "I don't see color" must sound ridiculous to a young child who is processing all the different shades of skin surrounding them. Your child is already noticing differences in race and culture; go ahead and embrace these differences. Teaching a Black kid to be color-blind can be dangerous for their physical and emotional safety when they grow up; in addition, it will not lead to anti-racist action in their future because color-blindness implies that acknowledging race is a bad thing. Let them do what comes naturally, but be ready to teach them that differences don't mean someone is superior or inferior. It is okay to say, "Wow, Abby's hair is purple" if Abby has purple hair. Abby's hair can be just as beautiful as everyone else's. If another parent says, "I don't see color," correct them. You don't want your child to buy any of that nonsense.

It is okay to start explaining to your child that they are Black. Your child will grow up appreciating their own beauty if they can see that they are unique, and yet fit into a group. They might get confused or not understand what you're trying to teach them at first, particularly if they're mixed-race and defy what some would consider "easy labeling." Ask lots of questions about what they see in the course of the day. Be patient, start with small steps, and have fun!

Make actively anti-racist choices as a consumer

It can be hard to teach a child that Black is beautiful if they see no representations of Blackness in their environment. Books with strong, positive, and diverse characters are great tools for encouraging your child's recognition and celebration of differences, but go even further. Your child is picking up cues from even just the packaging on his or her cereal box. Look for packaging that reflects a diversity in order to prevent your child from thinking that the world should celebrate only one skin color. It might seem like a small step, but every little bit counts. Do some research! If you're looking for Black dolls that really represent your child, know that *Essence* Magazine recently published "We Found the Black Dolls Your Little Ones Will Love Forever." Looking for skin care products for your teenager? Google Black-owned brands dedicated to Black skin.

Practice talking about race, even if you're not confident

Now is the time to start practicing the process of posing questions to your child about race; it will lead you to more fruitful conversations as they grow, and help them establish a foundational level of trust with you. Ask them what they saw today or what they are feeling. Kids in this age group are so focused on having their needs met that you must prompt them for other topics of discussion. You may not have a lot to talk about in regard to race specifically at this age, but using race-conscious language with them will help prepare them for a future as an anti-racist who can stand on their own and advocate for themselves.

Chicago Parent[19] shared a list of creative activities that can be used to start the conversation early with your kids. These hands-on learning activities and crafts, which focus on diversity and anti-racism, include the M&M Experiment, M is for Melanin, Brown =♥, Paper Doll Dress Up, Wooden Rainbow People, The Colors of Me, Matching Hearts, Diversity Princess Activity, and Self-Portrait.

Model the world you want your child to see

Many parents plan play dates and other activities for their children. Try as best you can to find diverse playmates for your kid—playmates who are of color, but also playmates who are non-Black. This is also a good time for you to check your own prejudice, and consider your own peer group: Expand it so that your own circle of friends is filled with vibrant, diverse people who can support you as you learn to parent, and teach you new things. Remember you're modeling the world for your child, so make it a world of inclusivity. If you only have Black or white friends, your child will notice. If you're Afro-Caribbean and you only mingle with light-skinned people, your child will notice. If you're Afro-Latinx and live in a bubble that doesn't include other Black individuals, yeah…your child will notice!

Model the values you want your child to have

During this early stage of development, the main challenge is to lay positive groundwork for later stages when your child has developed language skills and can more easily interact with you. Practice modeling compassion and tolerance, even when it is difficult. Racial tensions are almost palpable these days, and it can be so easy to see non-Black people as a monolith (and the source of all Black people's problems) and simply exclude them from your child's life. Be mindful of your own biases and behaviors and refrain from saying or doing things you would not want your child to mimic, including making

---

19   Chicago Parent (2020)

racist comments about other minority groups and telling jokes that disparage other races.

If you start out by making discussions about race a normal part of your child's nurturing while they are still in infancy and toddlerhood, you'll have an easier time as the child grows and the lessons become more difficult. This is a fun time in your child's life, though it can be challenging with temper tantrums and all the milestones your child is reaching. At this stage, you should spend a lot of time playing with your child and showing them the world you'd like them to ideally inhabit, one that is rich with diversity and celebrates their Blackness. Next, we'll look at the discussions and activities you should have with kids three to eleven years old, and how you can best help them build a foundation for their teenage years in terms of coping with racism and educating them about the concept.

Chapter 3

How to Talk to Young Children about Race (Pre-K and Elementary)

Young Children

Starting when they are very young, Black children are the subjects of racist attacks, not only by their peer group, but by adults. In 2017, a Georgia couple, Kayla Norton and Jose "Joe" Torres (and members of their cohort) were sentenced to prison for making armed threats at an eight-year-old Black child's outdoor birthday party. Earlier that day, the group had gone on a rampage through their county in a "celebration" of the Confederate flag.[20]

This kind of behavior is not just limited to the United States.[21] It's a global occurrence. The British National Society for the Prevention of Cruelty to Children reported that for 2017–2018 there were a total of 10,571 racially motivated attacks reported to British police authorities,

20 Chappell (2017)
21 Herbert (2005)

and that the rate of abuse had increased by about a thousand from the previous year.[22]

In June of 2020, three German men were arrested for attacking a mother and her three-year-old child in Dresden after the child was injured in the attack.[23] In England, The Black, Asian and Minority Ethnic Football Forum (BFF) reports that children as young as seven years old are subject to verbally racist attacks on British football pitches by white parents.[24]

In the United States, there have even been several incidents where children were punished or suspended from school for wearing their hair in ways that violated school dress codes, which penalizes Black children for how their hair grows naturally. DeAndre Arnold, a high school senior from Texas was told he couldn't walk at his graduation and receive his diploma in the graduation ceremony unless he cut off his dreadlocks.[25] School administrators in these cases often cite dress codes and other regulations as leading to the problem, but the rules should be changed if they are interfering in a child's ability to participate in school activities.

Stress caused by this kind of abuse can lead very young children to experience feelings of self-hatred, hopelessness and depression, and these can have tragic consequences. In 2018, nine-year-old McKenzie Adams committed suicide after a boy in her class repeatedly bullied her and attacked her with racist slurs in Alabama. Perhaps the hardest part of this story to grasp is that McKenzie's parents allegedly asked the school to intervene several times and were told that there was no problem. McKenzie was even disciplined for reporting the behavior, according to her family.[26]

---

22 Picheta (2019)
23 Three-year-old child injured in 'racist' assault in Dresden" (2020)
24 Bulman (2019)
25 Asmelash (2020)
26 Bonvillian (2020)

How to Talk with Your Child about Race during this Stage

Expose your kids to differences that are normal and celebrated

Create some opportunity for your child to step outside their egocentric worldview by introducing them to people who are different and are also willing to interact with your child in a positive manner. This will help them see beyond caricatured images of other groups of people and denounce racist situations they might find themselves in.

Beware of stereotypes

Children at this age are still struggling with abstract ideas and concepts and can't always see what is real and what is fictional. They may wholeheartedly believe in the Easter Bunny, but think a Native American is only real if they are in ceremonial garb with a headdress of feathers. Therefore, stereotypes and caricatures can be especially harmful to children at this stage. If you find your child is falling into stereotypical thought patterns, challenge the stereotype. Point out caricatures when you see them. For example, you might see a group photo of all-white astronauts and use it as an opportunity to teach them about Mae C. Jemison or Michael P. Anderson. "There are Black astronauts too!" Find creative ways of introducing Black notable figures into your child's classroom by helping them locate Black figures for school reports and homework.

My Afro-Caribbean friend Fabienne shared some tips with me: "[My son] Prose is learning to swim now, and we've been looking into Olympic swimmers. On the surface, almost everybody's white. But I told him, 'Let's look for some more swimmers,' and I deliberately showed him Simone Manuel. Now, he sees for himself someone who looks like him and can swim. I also do this for class assignments. Let's say his teacher wants him to find things that begin with the letter K. We bring pictures of Black kings in Africa, or Black karate students."

Consider feelings

Children at this age are developing the language to explain abstract concepts like emotions. Help your child become emotionally literate by asking what they are feeling. Feel free to express your own emotions too: "I feel sad when other people think you have to look a certain way to do some things (like be an astronaut)."

Bring the world home

Learn about other cultures and people by doing things like trying their cuisine or watching movies. Ask your child's teacher how much multiculturalism is built into the school curriculum and encourage them to foster a broader worldview. If you are bilingual, speak in your second language, and encourage your child to study and learn it as well. Even if you are not bilingual, learning a new language with your child is a valuable skill for both of you to have. When kids are exposed to other languages and cultures, they tend to become more accepting of others as they grow older.

Talk about how words and actions can hurt

Children at this stage are beginning to learn that words and actions can affect how other people feel. Check in with your child and explain to them that sometimes kids can be cruel and may bully them because of the tone of their skin. Let your child know they can come to you if they are picked on for being Black, or for any reason. If your child is being picked on, be prepared to help them by contacting the school on their behalf. Teach them how to be assertive and to self-advocate with their teachers. In Chapters 9 and 10, I provide you with the tools to help your children fight harmful behavior and language at school.

Talk about both the science and the social impact of skin color

Many people of color have a memory of having attention called to their skin color and being embarrassed. If you are direct in talking to your child about skin color, it will head off the embarrassment and pain of being surprised at being singled out. Many parents shush their kids if they point out differences like skin color or disability in public and ask questions, but it's perfectly natural for your child to want to understand. As best you can be direct and honest, "We have dark skin because of something called melanin in our skin. Everyone has it, but we have a little more."

For some pointers, watch on YouTube the Ted-Ed video by Angela Koine Flynn, "The Science of Skin Color." When ultraviolet sunlight hits our skin, it affects each of us differently. Depending on skin color, it'll take only minutes of exposure to turn one person beetroot-pink, while another requires hours to experience the slightest change. What's to account for that difference, and how did our skin come to take on so many different hues to begin with? Angela Koine Flynn answers by describing how the science of skin color works.

Point out examples of systemic racism

During this stage, your child is becoming increasingly aware of unfairness not just in their interactions with others, but with the people they may see in their environment. Ask questions of your child and encourage them to be aware of inequity. Your child may come to you and ask why none of their teachers are Black, for example. You might say, "It's not because white people are better at teaching. It's because it is harder for people with brown or Black skin to get a good paying job. It's not fair, and we are working as a family to change that." Explain it in terms of fairness, because that's a concept your child will understand and appreciate. Explain to them what inequality is. Maybe you ask them to remember when their little sister went out with an aunt and got ice cream, but no one else in the family did. However you explain unfairness to them, use age-appropriate language and examples.

Once they're older, you might want to give more specific examples of systemic racism. I recently shared the following story with my nineteen-year-old niece, which involves my internship at an affluent private school in Miami.

I was an education student, and my "field experience" became a full-blown internship because the teachers I assisted reported their amazement at how fun my lessons were, and how engaged I could get the most distractible first graders. I was also a team player, they said, and I do remember that particular year as one filled with laughter despite the fact that I held a full-time job AND a full-time internship and was always exhausted.

Every week, I had to check in on the phone with a veteran teacher selected by the university so she could provide guidance, and every other week or so, she'd visit me at the school to see me at work and evaluate my performance. She was always beaming with pride when she came to the school: I had potential. On that day, she was also amused: I was dressed in a chicken costume, having conducted an exciting lesson based on the story of a rooster named Jose.

When I expressed an interest in applying for the open position at the school, my mentor, a kind white woman in her seventies, took in a deep breath. "Michele," she said, "I need you to listen to me and listen to me carefully. They'll never hire you. You need to grow a thick skin and become keenly aware of your surroundings. Because you always give 100 percent of yourself, if you're not careful, they'll suck you dry."

She'd heard that I'd been volunteering in the morning and the afternoon at the car line; she'd heard I'd been tutoring a kid for free once a week. She'd also heard from the principal that parents had been calling the office, asking why a Black woman had been allowed into their children's classroom. ("She's just an intern," the principal had to reassure them.) She'd heard that some of these parents had used the N-word.

"I'm so sorry, Michele," she said. "You don't deserve the hate."

When I applied for the job anyway, the principal was also candid about the situation. She explained to me that I wasn't a good fit, and she, too, was surprised that I'd been so naïve about the realities of the world I'd walked in.

Obviously, a young child will not understand the complexities of this story. Stick to ice cream and fairness.

Elementary School

As they grow older, the abuse Black children suffer becomes more heated and violent. Black kids are subject to "adultification," or the perception that they are more mature than they are. They also become more vulnerable to abuse in many ways, as parents start to allow tweens more freedom and have less oversight over what happens when they are on their own, even for the most mundane tasks. In May of 2020, eleven-year-old Skhylur Davis, from South Carolina, was physically assaulted when a neighbor saw her gathering her grandmother's mail. The neighbor grabbed Skhylur and accused her of stealing her mail. The woman wasn't arrested but was charged with third degree assault.[27]

In September of 2019, two girls (ages ten and eleven) were charged with harassment and assault due to a hate crime, for an attack they launched on a ten-year-old Black girl who was called racist names and had her eye blackened.[28] The school bus monitor, who is white,

---

27 "SC Attorney Says Black 11 Year Old Was Victim of Racist Attack" (2020)
28 Associated Press (2019)

was also charged with endangering the welfare of a minor when they failed to intervene in the attack.

The British National Society for the Prevention of Cruelty to Children reports that Black kids in England as young as ten years old are whitening their skin to fend off racist abuse (Picheta, 2019).

In Ottawa, Canada, in February of 2020, ten-year-old Bella Etaka was assaulted by classmates who punched her, spat on her, and called her a "nigger." They told her that her hair looked like a "blackbird's nest," and that her skin looked like "cow shit." Bella's mother, Agnes said, "My reaction was anger. Frustration. Pain. Deep pain. I felt like I had failed to protect my kid. I felt like the system had failed my child, the school had failed my child. And I just cried. Let's call it what it is. It's a hate crime. They assaulted my kid on the school bus." Ms. Ataka said she was speaking out in the hopes that it would draw more attention to the problem. This wasn't the first time Bella had been attacked because of her race. Her mother had already taken Bella out of another school because of racist bullying.[29]

How to Talk with Your Child about Race during this Stage

Understand how your child views the world

As they progress through elementary school, children become more aware of groups and cliques, and who belongs and who does not belong to different groups. They are eager to learn more about their own group and how to publicly express affiliation with that group as their identity and pride in connection to the group grows. They begin to seek role models (from within their group) that they can identify with. Kids at this age are also becoming more aware of racism against

---

29   Cotnam (2020)

their group. You may find that personal prejudice is becoming an integral part of your child's attitude and may see them act upon it. Name-calling and bullying are two common ways personal racism is expressed at this age.

Ask questions and let your kids ask questions too

You don't need to have any fancy qualifications to start discussing racism with your kid. You can talk to them about racism in a practical way that reflects their growing experiences with the problem. Children pick up a lot more than we realize, and kids in this age group are especially curious. Focus the conversations on questions you ask each other and be prepared to listen to their answers. Listening shows your child that you care about their opinion and experiences. Let them tell you how they see things before you offer any information, because it will help you understand what your child has already faced. You don't even need to make this a formal talk.

If you need some materials, the Anti-Defamation League[30] (www.adl. org) provides fun activities and opportunities to talk with children (ages three to twelve) about respect, inclusion, diversity, bias and social justice. Each activity is followed by discussion prompts for talking with children about what they learned, their feelings and any questions they might have.

Validate their feelings

Children in this age group can express their emotions clearly, and their feelings about racism are growing in complexity during this same stage as they develop cultural pride and political awareness. The burden of directing the conversation isn't something you need to take on. You'll be able to listen and validate your children's feelings better if you let them co-lead the discussion. If they don't volunteer how

---

30   "Thinking about Social Justice through Crafts and Conversation" (2020)

they feel about racism as it pertains to their personal experiences, you should ask them how they feel. This will let them know their feelings are natural and that they are understood. It also creates a safe space for your child to process the many complicated emotions that racism can kick up.

Continue to be an advocate

Talk to your kids about what is and is not fair. Children this age are developing a deeper moral sensibility that lends itself well to discussions about how to disrupt prejudice and racist attitudes when they encounter it. For example, you can tell them, "I don't think it's fair that people say Black men make the best football players because it reinforces a stereotype that Black men are only good at some things." Your child will learn the vocabulary of disruption from these chats.

Teach them about perspective and help them navigate confusing messages

Children need help understanding the difference between acknowledging cultural differences and stereotyping or creating caricatures. They also need help understanding the difference between "majority" and "minority" viewpoints. Understanding that people can have a difference of opinion will help keep your child from taking harmful majority views personally.

Kids this age will also begin to see biased views from people within your friend and family circle that can be confusing to them. For example, Grandma uses a homophobic slur at dinner. Your child is confused. He has a strong relationship with his grandmother, but her words are completely out of line with what you've taught your child. First, directly speak to your parent about their homophobic attitude, even if it's in front of your child. Address it as soon as possible: "Grandma loves us and we love her, but what she said was wrong.

We don't discriminate against people. Grandma needs to do better than that."[31]

Don't make light of Grandma's comment and simply call it a "different viewpoint." I suggest you keep in mind James Baldwin's quote, "We can disagree and still love each other unless your disagreement is rooted in my oppression and denial of my humanity and right to exist." In other words, racism and homophobia, for example, are more than just a disagreement on viewpoint; they are rooted in the denial of humanity. How can we teach children to be anti-racist, and at the same time chalk this up to Grandma's "different viewpoint"? Grandma is wrong. Say it. This prepares children for the friends or coworkers or bosses who will claim to love them but also hold racist views. What kind of love would this be?

Teach them history

Children at this age are developing an understanding of history and geography and how they tie into cultural and racial identity through ancestry. This allows your child to develop a more complex understanding of the history of racism, how it began as a social and institutional construction, and how it is still impacting society as it has for hundreds of years. That will help prevent them from internalizing any racist behavior they may be experiencing, and allow them to have a broader understanding of the scope of the issue, that it isn't just a modern problem. Watching films and documentaries about the history of slavery will educate them further. Also teach your children about the history before history, so they understand that slavery was not the beginning of their cultural heritage and that they have roots in a continent of culture and a people who have accomplished great things. Teach them about discrimination against other groups too, like the history of Native American decimation,

---

31   Arnold-Ratliff (2020)

and how these systems continue to operate through reservations, and about other inequities.

Continue to have conversations about structural and systemic racism

The conversations you had with your child in preschool about systemic racism and issues like pay disparity, incarceration rates, lack of educational support, and so forth are ones that should continue through elementary school. Keep letting your child know it's not a fair system and that it can be dismantled with hard work and determination, but that it is much more complicated than individual attitudes. This is a good time in your child's life to start introducing them to the political process as well. Discuss people running for local government positions and discuss issues the candidates address in their platforms. This will lead your child into an understanding of civic engagement.

Create change

You can help your child feel enabled to help dismantle racism by taking small steps with them during these years.[32] Suggest they research an historical event by doing an internet search with them or visit the library together and find books on the issue or even conduct interviews with people you know could help them learn more about history. Explain to them that knowledge is powerful and that sharing knowledge with others makes a difference and can change people's minds and actions. It is important that your child not think they have to dismantle racism single-handedly, so start with small steps and let them see that others are engaged in making real change happen in the hopes that future generations will enjoy a racist-free society. Let them know the problem is more than just about personal prejudices, that

---

32   Feris (2015)

it's woven into the fabric of our society and has been handed down for centuries.

Throughout this book, I'll share the story of Brian Cooks, who opened up about his experiences with racism in a poignant (and public) Facebook post that went viral, where he clearly illustrates the toll racism takes on a person, from childhood to adulthood. Here, Brian relates his experiences during elementary school in Naperville, Illinois:

"In elementary school, I was in the gifted program. I've never been any good at math or science, but I was a really creative kid who loved history and telling stories. In third grade, the gifted program focused on the Middle Ages. I was in heaven. I loved learning about knights and castles and all that stuff. We had a group project to do some time that year, where we had to give a short speech about something we'd learned during the year. All the groups broke off to divvy up the work, when my teacher came over to my group. Wouldn't it be "easier" and more fun for me if my group did our presentation as a rap? I'm eight years old. I have no history writing any kind of music, much less a full three or four minutes of rap verses for me and my teammates. But I tried. The other kids just expected it to be natural for me. They looked at me like, "What do you mean you don't know how to rap?" We ended up just doing it as a regular presentation like everybody else, and afterward my teacher came up to me and said, "I thought you guys were going to rap? I was looking forward to MC Brian." Again, she didn't know that she was making a racially insensitive statement. Why would she? It's not like she'd had deep conversations about how Black people feel about their Blackness, or the way Black people internalized the way white people feel about our Blackness."

How Racism Harms Children

It is a "no-brainer" that racism affects Black children, but the professionals have also weighed in on the issue. In 2019, The

American Academy of Pediatrics issued a policy statement that referred to racism as a "socially transmitted disease," in part, because children in minority groups are subject to chronic stress. They noted that higher levels of chronic stress lead to changes in stress hormones, which leads to inflammation, which is a marker for chronic diseases and autoimmune disorders like heart disease, asthma and diabetes. Furthermore, changes to a mother's level of stress hormones during pregnancy can infect her developing infant, leading to higher infant mortality risk and lower birth weights.[33]

Minority children are more likely to live in lower income homes with greater rates of unemployment, which can impact their access to quality healthcare, education, and decent housing. But the problem of racism is still present in higher income communities, where minority children are more likely to be punished at school, and less likely to be offered special education for learning disabilities. Teachers are also more likely to underestimate minority kids, which doesn't give them the needed impetus to push harder and try to achieve more. They are more likely to be suspended for behavior problems and have a higher rate of absenteeism.[34] In the 2016–2017 school year, 89 percent of white students graduated high school, while only 78 percent of their Black classmates earned a degree. And of those students entering college in 2011, 64 percent of white students, but only 40 percent of Black students earned a bachelor's degree after six years.[35]

---

33   McCarthy (2019)
34   Anderson (2015)
35   "The Impact of Racism on Children's Health" (2020)

Chapter 4

How to Talk to Your Tweens and Teens about Race

A lot happens in this last age group (ages eleven and up) as far as development goes. While children in this stage have reached an age where they can fully grasp abstract concepts and ideas, can formulate strategy, and can express their emotions clearly, they are also subject to the flood of hormones that comes with hitting puberty, and are often trying to gain autonomy and independence from their parents, which can lead to some serious power struggles and disagreements. Depending on what stage they are in, you may also find that your tweens and teenagers are all over the place emotionally, which can make having a fruitful discussion difficult. Do it anyway, because at this stage, having "the Talk" becomes more important than ever.

This is a particularly vulnerable stage for your child. As they gain the independence they may be seeking, and learn to do things like drive, they also become more likely to be stopped and questioned by police officers or become victims to a crime. This can be a scary stage for parents, who are also learning what it means exactly to parent a teenager, and may still feel a strong impulse to protect their child, while simultaneously preparing for them to leave home and go to college or enter the workforce.

It can often feel like there's just no easy way to communicate with a teenager, but remembering to be patient will help. You're learning too, and the discussions you have with your teens will be a lot more complicated than the ones you had with them when they were infants—if you can get them talking.

Parents should encourage middle school children to ask questions

Check on them and see how they are feeling before you begin a discussion. You may need to change what you want to talk about based on their emotional state, but knowing that they have a voice in the discussion and that you are listening will help them open up. They'll appreciate that they have a safe place to process their emotions about difficult conversations. Take an interest in what your child is watching on television or in the media. It's a good idea to watch with them, but you can also ask them to talk about what they've been watching. If they mention a YouTube video you haven't seen, ask them to show it to you, and then discuss it with them. However, be prepared to say you can't watch something with them if the content is too disturbing in your opinion. In this age, viral videos of violent deaths like the murder of George Floyd are being disseminated over the internet, and your child may see one before they realize what they are watching. They may not know how to handle that level of violence. It's difficult for an adult to watch, let alone a child. Let them know you understand that they are upset at the video, that it is shocking and disturbing, and that many people are upset by it. If they seem especially upset, offer to seek out a grief counselor to help you navigate the discussion.

You can also watch these seven-minute interviews with twelve-year-olds reflecting on their identities (www.wnyc.org/story/people-sometimes-think-im-supposed-talk-ghetto-whatever-kids-race). Ask your child which kids they felt had an interesting story and why.

Ask questions too

Direct inquiries to a teenager sometimes don't hit their mark. Typical response: "I dunno." Part of getting a response from your teenager is learning how to ask the right questions. Ask them where they see unfair situations in their own lives or in those of their classmates and friends. You'll probably get a little further with a teenager if you aren't preaching to them about what's right and wrong, and spend more time listening. Let them come to their own understanding of the larger social impact of what they are telling you. At this age, children are capable of abstract thought and will better understand racism, injustice, and the difference between civil disobedience and violent protest. They will be more likely to talk it through with you if they know you care to hear what they think.

One good tool to get your child answering questions about their thinking on race is "Why Color Blindness Will NOT End Racism" (www.youtube.com/watch?v=H4LpT9TF_ew). It's about six minutes long. After watching the YouTube video, you can talk about these questions: What makes people think race is a biological trait? If race is a social construct and was invented by society to categorize people, why does it matter? In the video, three different examples of structural racism are discussed. Can you summarize them in your own words? Why should people NOT claim to be blind to racial differences?

Remember that teenagers often fail to see things in their full complexity

Kids at this stage are beginning to really value their identity and are laying down a solid foundation for adulthood. Most kids will choose to lead a life where they are accepting of differences and will choose to act with compassionate respect for their fellow human beings. Some, unfortunately, will choose a much darker way of life. If you see or hear your child speaking with bias or hate speech—whether in person or on social media—say something. Remember though that adolescents are still forming a solid set of values, and it might be better to ask questions. Tell them: We're not on the same page with this. What do *you* believe? And then be prepared to add some nuance to their argument, because they are often missing out on the subtleties of the situation and they react from a place of emotional intensity with a reduction in logical reasoning. They may, for example, start talking in generalities about white people as all racist. Remind them there are white allies even if the system is skewed in favor of whites. Bring some logic back into the discussion and stay calm. These discussions can be scary and intense, and you can take a break to find some composure if needed. Understand that your child is still learning.

You can watch three short films on implicit bias and racism from Film Shorts on Bias (NYTimes) (www.nytimes.com/video/who-me-biased) which discusses different aspects of racism, how it develops, and ways to comprehend and deal with it.

Help them develop media literacy

While it's important to listen to your adolescent, it is also helpful to introduce them to historical precedent. Show them images of protests or videos of marches, because let's face it, they are nothing new, and the history of protest is an important legacy to hand down to your kids. This is also a good time to start talking to your kids about critical thinking and media literacy, because there is a lot of misinformation out there. Tell them, "Oh, that's fascinating, where did you learn about that?" Remember, you are helping them to develop independent thinking skills they will need as they mature into adults. If you want them to be people who make a difference in the world, then shepherd them in that direction gently.

Avoid stereotypes

If your child is buying into stereotypes, complicate their thinking by pointing out the nuances that exist behind the oversimplification caused by stereotyping. It can be difficult to convince a teenager to take a second look at something they have set in their ways, so let them know you have an opinion about what they think. Tell them: "What you are saying sounds disrespectful to me." Or, say, "I used to see things the way you are looking at them, but then I saw_____ or read _____, and it changed my mind." Even if it feels like you are getting no reaction, your kid is at least hearing what you are trying to tell them.

One good way to root out stereotypical thinking, even if it's not conscious, is to take the Implicit Associations Test(s) at implicit. harvard.edu/implicit/education.html. These anonymous online tests measure implicit bias toward different groups of people. Some of the tests include: Age, Disability, Race, Gender, etc. These tests are good at measuring implicit bias, which your teen might not even be aware they have.

Encourage activism

Kids at this age want to feel like they have some agency in affecting change. Learning about racism but having nothing to do about it can lead to frustration, and maybe even into dangerous behaviors. Wanting to act is a powerful impulse; you'll want to teach them how best to channel their energy in a positive direction. Introduce them to local organizations in your area that are anti-racist, like your local Black Lives Matter group or an after-school community center program that is invested in social justice. Get involved yourself by marching, donating to a cause or otherwise organizing in your local community. This will also help them feel less alone, and less scared, because they will meet other people who are actively fighting against racism in a positive way. Walk "the talk." Teenagers are great at giving the eye roll to just about anything you tell them during this stage. But you are more likely to earn their respect by modeling behavior you want them to emulate. So, get involved with local or national organizations working to change things, and invite your child to join you. You'll be supporting a generation who is desperate to see real, effective, lasting change.

Give Them "the Talk"

I've mentioned a few times already that "the Talk" is never about one discussion; it's a series of conversations you will have with your child over the course of their lives. Now is probably the most important time in their lives to continue having the Talk because you'll want to keep them safe at a particularly vulnerable phase of their development. They may look like adults in many ways to people they encounter, but are still immature in many ways, and are beginning to better understand the implications of living in a system that has little if any respect for who they are, what they want to do, or their right to move freely and unfettered. Unfortunately, no matter how many times you have these conversations, there is no guarantee your child will remain safe, because many people will see them as a threat, even if they aren't doing anything more than relaxing at home or taking a jog. Keep having the conversation anyway.

In this excerpt of Brian Crooks' story, which he publicly shared on Facebook, he relates the frustration of being hassled by the police regularly:

I got pulled over a lot in high school. Like, a lot a lot. By this point, I was no longer driving the Dodge. I had a Mazda of my own. It was flashy and loud, but this was 2002 and everybody with a Japanese car was doing a Vin Diesel impression, so it's not like mine stood out that much more than anyone else's. I spent a ton of money on my car and was especially aware of its appearance. You can understand, then, why it was weird that I was routinely pulled over for a busted taillight. After all, that's the kind of thing I would've noticed and gotten fixed, especially if that taillight tended to burn out once a week or so.

My parents had told me how to act when pulled over by the police, so of course I was all "Yes sir, no sir" every time it happened. That didn't stop them from asking me to step out of the car so they could pat me down or search for drugs, though. I didn't have a drop of alcohol until I was twenty-one, but by that point I was an expert at breathalyzers and field sobriety tests. On occasion, the officer was polite. But usually, they walked up with their hand on their gun and talked to me like I'd been found guilty of a grisly homicide earlier in the day. A handful of times, they'd tell me to turn off the car, drop the keys out the window, and keep my hands outside the vehicle before even approaching.

Give them space to practice talking too

A key part of the process of relieving the stress of being Black is having a safe, conducive environment to vent frustrations. If your child comes to you and tells you about a racist encounter they had, encourage them to say all the things they couldn't say during the encounter. Let them yell if they want to. Then ask them, "What might have happened if you had said all those things at the time? How did you handle it?"

Use talk as a stress release valve. Probably for more than any other age group, the need to have a safe verbal outlet to relieve stress is important for teenagers. And let's face it, being Black in this world is stressful. No words can stop a trigger-happy cop from firing, but talking about that may help your child feel like they are dropping a heavy load. The more your child can get out their frustrations in a safe environment, the better able they will be to hold it together when they need to remain calm and focused on the situation at hand and do the things they need to do to remain safe. You'll feel better too, knowing they can come to you and let it out.

Continue talking about history

During this stage of their lives, history becomes much easier for children to grasp, and they can see where activism has led to change. Show them documentaries and films that will give them a foundation of understanding not just about history, but about how actions lead directly to consequences, both good and bad.

Here, Brian Crooks writes about the painful experience of dating in high school:

> In high school, I was around more Black kids. Still not a lot, but more than zero, so that was nice. When I was fifteen, I got my first 'real' girlfriend. I'd asked some girls out before, and some of them said yes, but when you're thirteen or fourteen years old, what does 'going out' even mean? So, my first 'real' girlfriend was white. After all, I was living in an overwhelmingly white community and it's not like I was a heartthrob, so I was in no position to tell a girl who liked me that

I was only interested in dating a Black girl. I might've never had a girlfriend if that was the line I drew. We were a good couple. We got along well and had similar interests and stuff. Basically, what you'd like to have as a high school sophomore. Her parents were divorced, but her mom and stepdad liked me. Then, her biological father found out I was Black. A week later, she called me crying and said we had to break up. Her dad didn't support her dating a Black person. So, my first heartbreak came as a direct result of racism.

An FAQ for Talking to Your Tweens and Teens about Racism

Parents of children in this age group may find that, quite often, they either aren't sure how to react to the things their children say or question how to handle reactions from their kids. There are plenty of resources to help you navigate the Talk online and in the resource guide that follows this chapter, but here are a few of the most common questions and some answers.

What do I say if, during a conversation, my child says something racist?

It can be alarming and shocking to hear your Black kid spout off something racist and nonsensical, and your first reaction may be to lose your temper. Rather than reacting in judgment or anger, ask questions. Treat the matter with curiosity, but also with seriousness. Ask them to repeat themselves. Ask them why they said what they said. Ask them where they learned that. Listen to what they tell you, and offer them more information that will deepen their understanding of why racist thinking and speech are problematic, no matter where they come from. Complicate any stereotypes they offer you.

Remember not to get defensive. Stay calm. Count to ten before you react if you are especially upset. Even the most progressive parents have kids who say things that shock them. Remember also, at this stage, your kid is trying to fit in with their peer group and may be mimicking something they heard elsewhere. This is a good time to check yourself and see if you may have reacted to something in a biased manner. If you have, let them know you regret saying that, and be more careful in the future. Ask your child where they learned what they said, and tell them, "I know many people think that way, but I don't and here's why…"

I know I make it sound like a very simple and easy thing to do for a parent. It's not. In today's climate where stereotypes can be extremely dangerous, I want to reiterate the fact that your tone should remain grave. I think of cases where kids regurgitate ideas about Muslims, about Asians, and even about themselves (think Kanye West and Candace Owen). As a parent, this would really hurt and alarm you. So how do you stay calm? Organizations like Race Forward (RaceForward.com) or Repair the World (WeRepair.org) offer free conversation guides to help you create an open, nonadversarial environment to talk about racism, racial equity, and racial healing with friends, family, colleagues and neighbors. If you want to read books to/with the children in your life that affirm the identities and backgrounds of *all* children, know that the American Library Association has curated a Unity, Kindness and Peace Reading List.

To broaden your child's understanding, you can watch Ta-Nehisi Coates on "Words That Don't Belong to You" which discusses whether white people should use the "n" word. (www.youtube.com/watch?time_continue=1&v=QO15S3WC9pg&feature=emb_logo)

If my child says they are afraid or angry, what do I say?

Start by validating your child's feelings. You may have similar feelings. Tell them, "I'm afraid and angry also. It's upsetting to see or hear about these things. Racism is unfair. But I feel better knowing that there are people who are working to change the situation in the world, and I remind myself that my energy is best channeled in that direction." Offer some examples of how people are trying to make change happen, whether it's in your community or on the national or international stage. Talk about what members of your family have done or are doing. It's helpful for kids to have role models.

The most important thing is to not minimize their anger or hurt or to make them feel they are irrational in feeling deeply about anything. But be sure you can offer them ways to express their emotions in a healthy, positive manner whether it is activism, or journaling, or exercising to release the extra energy from their systems. You can also offer to help them find a counselor to help them learn how to manage their emotions. Normalize therapy for them by letting them know that good mental hygiene is an essential part of being a happy person.

Trayvon Martin's death brought to attention the danger that Black teenagers face in doing things as simple as walking home from a convenience store, but the attention, unfortunately, hasn't brought about the necessary change needed to ensure our Black teenagers are safe from harm. Fourteen-year-old Emmett Till's murder in the 1950s drew the same sort of attention, again, a boy running a day-to-day errand to a store, again, with no lasting effect on the number of hate crimes committed against teenagers. It is a situation that can make the parent of a Black child feel powerless.

In June of 2020, two white men, Michael and Matthew Lemelin, were arrested after a racial attack on three teenage Black boys, ages thirteen, fourteen, and fifteen. The three boys were riding their bicycles in Manchester, Connecticut, on their way to buy diapers for a friend's child, when they were called racial slurs and nearly run down with one of their assailants' vehicles. The two men then chased down the boys and stole one of their bicycles.[36]

Remember:

1. All parents should talk to their kids about racism.[37]

2. Be honest, and do some self-examination. When talking about racism, it's important for you to keep a handle on your own biases or prejudices.

3. Keep a diverse library in your home with age-appropriate books about racism. Network with other parents and share resources with them.

4. Always allow your children to ask you anything, even if you don't have all the answers because silence will not protect you or them.[38]

5. Let your kids know their lives matter, and encourage them to forge their own identities.

6. This isn't easy. You may trip yourself up trying to find the right words to express what you mean to say. But listen to your gut. You probably know your child better than anyone else does and have an understanding of what they can handle. You don't have to pretend that dealing with racism is easy. It's okay for you to model how to cope for your kid, and you can only really do that if you have to cope with something yourself.

---

36   Leavenworth (2020)

37   McDermott (2020)

38   Dastagir (2020)

7. Keep a fair balance. Talking about racism isn't just about predicting what could happen and how to keep safe or recounting all of the awful things that have happened. Make sure that you are offering your kid some hope by showing them how things have already changed, and how people continue to work toward change in the future. Mention that there are allies out there and that there is a whole community of support for them to draw strength from.

Parent Resources

Books Recommendations

For Small Children

- *Something Happened in our Town: A Child's Story About Racial Injustice*, by Marianne Celano, Phd (Ages four to eight)
- *Daddy, There's a Noise Outside*, by Kenneth Braswell (Ages six and up)

These books can also lead to conversations with children on the topic of race and injustice:

- *I am Jackie Robinson*, by Brad Meltzer (Ages four to seven)
- *Let's Talk About Race*, by Julius Lester (Ages four to seven)
- *The Other Side*, by Jacqueline Woodson (Ages five to eight)
- *Viola Desmond Won't Be Budged*, by Jody Nyasha Warner (Ages eight to nine)
- *Separate is never equal: Sylvia Mendez and Her Family's Fight for Desegregation*, by Duncan Tonatiuh (Ages six to nine)

Here are some other books with diverse characters:

- *What's the Difference? Being Different is Amazing,* by Doyin Ridchards, Feiwel and Friends (Ages two to ten)
- *All the Colors We Are,* by Katie Kissinger (Ages three and up)
- *The Courageous Adventures of the Konscious Kidz,* by John Casselberry and Madeline Connor (Ages six to eleven)

For Young Adults (Grades 5–12)

- *All American Boys,* by Jason Reynolds
- *Dear Martin,* by Nic Stone
- *(The) Hate You Give,* by Angie Thomas
- *Ghost Boys,* by Jewell Parker Rhodes
- *On the Come Up,* by Angie Thomas
- *Stamped,* by Jason Reynolds and Ibram X. Kendi

For Teens

- *New Kid,* by Jerry Craft
  This graphic novel follows seventh grader Jordan Banks and his journey as the new kid at a prestigious private school. Jordan is one of the few kids of color in his entire grade.

- *March,* by John Lewis, Andrew Aydin, and Nate Powell
  March is a firsthand account of John Lewis's struggle for civil and human rights.

- *This Book is Anti-Racist,* by Tiffany Jewell, illustrated by Aurelia Durand.
  In this book for the young person who doesn't know how to speak up against racial injustice, Jewell writes about racism and how to undo it.

For High School Students and for Parents

Books to learn about racism in the United States

- *Between the World and Me,* by Ta-Nehisi Coates
- *How to Be an Antiracist,* by Ibram X. Kendi
- *Black Stats: African Americans by the Numbers in the Twenty-first Century,* by Monique W. Morris
- *The Invention of the White Race,* by Theodore W. Allen
- *The New Jim Crow: Mass Incarceration in the Age of Colorblindness,* by Michelle Alexander
- *So You Want to Talk About Race,* by Ijeoma Oluo
- *Tears We Cannot Stop: A Sermon to White America,* by Michael Eric Dyson
- *White Fragility: Why It's So Hard for White People to Talk About Racism,* by Robin DiAngelo
- *White Rage: The Unspoken Truth of Our Racial Divide,* by Carol Anderson, PhD
- *Your Black Friend and Other Strangers,* by Ben Passmore

Check out "These Books Can Help You Explain Racism and Protest to Your Kids," a list curated by *The New York Times* (www.nytimes.com/2020/06/02/parenting/kids-books-racism-protest.html). *PBS* also has a recommended reading list, plus a hub of resources for middle and high school students.

Book Lists

- *Good Housekeeping* and *PBS Kid*s also have lists of kids' books that can help start the conversation about race. Social Justice Books (socialjusticebooks.org) offers a valuable selection of multicultural and social justice books for children, YA, and educators, including Afro-Latinx titles.

- The Brown Bookshelf (thebrownbookshelf.com) has a collection of books that include brown and Black protagonists who deal at times with tough issues, and Common Sense Media (a nonprofit that rates movies, TV shows, books, apps and other media for parents and schools) has curated a list of eighty books with diverse, multicultural characters for kids of all ages (www.commonsensemedia.org/lists/books-with-characters-of-color).

- Check out this list by *The New York Times*: www.nytimes.com/2020/06/03/parenting/kids-books-racism.html.

Other Resources

YouTube videos

- *The Story of Ruby Bridges*, by Robert Coles (Ages three and up)
- *Child of the Civil Rights Movement*, by Paula Young Shelton (Ages four to eight)
- *The Stone Thrower*, by Joel Ealey Richardson (Ages four to nine)
- *Rosa*, by Nikki Giovanni (Age eight to ten)

I also recommend:

- Sesame Street: *Color of Me*
- Sesame Street: *What I Am*
- Sesame Street: *I Love My Hair* (bilingual)
- *Jump Shamador* (activist song)

Also:

- The website Raising Equity provides free videos and resources on how parents can fight racism and cultivate an open mind in themselves and their kids

- Watch *Eyes on the Prize*, the award-winning PBS documentary chronicling the history of civil rights

Other Videos and Read-A-Loud Books

- *Back of the Bus*, by Aaron Reynolds
- *Bippity Bop Barbershop*, by Natasha Anastasia Tarpley
- *The Case for Loving—The Fight for Interracial Marriage— Words on Screen*
- *Don't Touch My Hair!* by Sharee Miller
- *Feast for 10*, by Cathryn Falwell
- *Henry's Freedom Box*, by Ellen Levine
- *Hair Love*, a full short film by Sony Pictures Animation
- *I Am Enough*, by Grace Byers
- *Let the Children March*, by Monica Clark-Robinson
- *Moses*, by Carole Boston Weatherford
- *The Story of Ruby Bridges*, by Robert Coles

Toys

For toys, check out:

- People Colors Crayon Pack
- Sugarfoot Rag Dolls
- Pattycake Doll Company

Chapter 5

Activism and Allyship

Ways to Safely Engage in Activism

With images of unrest and violence surrounding protests prevalent in the media, you may be hesitant to take your children to a protest, and it may not be the right activity for your particular child. While the majority of protests are peaceful marches and vigils for justice, depending on the age of your kids, it may not be ideal to take them to one right now. Whatever form your child's activism takes, it is important that they have an understanding of why people protest and the impact it can have. Without protests and acts of civil disobedience, there might not have been any of the advances we have made in the fight against racism: No Civil Rights Act, no voter protection. We might still be living under Jim Crow laws. Representative John Lewis, the civil rights champion who marched in Selma and throughout the South, and in Washington, DC, once said, "You only pass this way once, you gotta give it all you can." It will take many people giving their all to make the world a better place. Encourage your child to be part of the movement in whatever way they can contribute.

But activism isn't limited to protests about racism; there are plenty of causes worth fighting for, some of which intersect with anti-racist protests. There are many activities you can encourage your child to take part in that make a difference. There are also plenty of young activists, like the ones mentioned in this chapter, who find ways to fight racism and for other causes on their own terms, using their own methods.[39]

Educate and read: When she was fourteen years old, Marley Dias became frustrated at the lack of representation of children of color in the books she was reading. She penned her own children's book, *Marley Dias Gets It Done: And So Can You*, started her own zine on elle.com, and started the #1000BlackGirlBooks drive. She has been vocal about calling out publishers on their lack of representation of people of color in the books they publish.[40]

Attend a town hall: Many Black kids have attended town hall meetings and there are several Black youth town halls that meet virtually over the world wide web. Fifteen-year-old Kayla Cocci attended a town hall hosted by Public Citizens for Children and Youth.[41] She writes: "I am a product of the love that we lack in today's society. My skin color is the outcome of the unity between white and black love. I have also been put in an awful position by my own brothers and sisters. I watch mortified with the reminder that my Black brother could be Trayvon Martin, I cry with tears of frustration that my white grandparents who have raised me stare at their own race with anger, and with fear of the evil that they could do to women and men who look like their granddaughter and grandson. My skin is one color, but my heart is divided because of society."

Advocate for Legislation/Engage civically: When she was just eight years old, Mari Copeny wrote to then-President Barack Obama about the polluted water crisis in Flint, Michigan and requested that he travel to Flint to attend hearings being held and see firsthand the

39 Fitzpatrick (2017)
40 Wicker (2019)
41 Kim (2020)

devastation the tainted water supply was bringing to her community. To her surprise, the president not only responded to her letter, he also traveled to Flint, and as a result of his visit, authorized $150 million in aid to help repair the water system.[42] Mari continues to work with activists in Flint, passing out water filters and advocating for clean water supplies and doing other community activism in her hometown.[43]

Run for office: While most races require a minimum age of eighteen for candidates to be eligible to run for office, you can show your kids role models that will encourage them to run for office when they reach the age of maturity. For example, Congresswoman Ilhan Omar is the first naturalized citizen, the first Somali-American, and the first woman of color to hold office in Minnesota. Her daughter Isra Hirsi is a Black environmental activist and founded the US Youth Climate Strike.

Protest: Naomi Wadler was eleven years old when she took the stage at the March for Our Lives Rally in Washington, DC, and spoke about Black women who have died in gun violence. Her speech added a necessary element of intersectionality to the gun debate which is often centered on the deaths of white males.

If you do go to a protest, here are several tips to help you keep your kid safe:[44]

1. **Stick together.** Make sure your kids know that they'll likely be in a crowd and that they will have to stay with you throughout the protest. Also, stick to the outer perimeter of the protest. The epicenter of a protest can have large throngs of jostling people— not the best place for a kid. Stick to the outskirts of the protest

42   Burton (2019)
43   Wicker (2019)
44   Bregel (2020)

where there's more room to move around and you'll still be able to be part of the action and have your voice heard, but you'll also be able to take a break and sit down if your kids are tired.

2. **Plan events wisely.** Do a little research to find out who is sponsoring the protest and whether or not it is family-friendly; some protests are specifically geared toward family participation. Bring enough bottled water for everyone as it can get hot at a protest, especially during the warm summer months, and protests can be all day affairs. Don't forget your chargers in case your cell phones run out of battery power.

3. **Write your cell phone number on your kid's arm.** In the event that your child is separated from you, someone will be able to call you. Even if your child is old enough to memorize your number, write it on their arm in case of an emergency.

4. **Dress your kid for comfort.** Make sure your kid is wearing closed-toe, comfortable walking shoes. Pack sunscreen and hats and make sure their clothing is appropriate for the weather conditions.

5. **Pace yourselves.** It's important not to overdo it at protests. You're going to make sure your voices are heard and that you are represented along with a crowd of other people. You don't have to attend the whole day-long event. Especially the first few times you go, you'll want to pay attention to your kid's comfort level and make sure they are safe and happy.

Create a public awareness campaign that includes social media / Pick up the digital pen: By the age of fifteen, Winter BreeAnne founded the advocacy organization Black is Lit to encourage more Black representation on Instagram.[45] Her campaign quickly gained national attention. Since then, she has joined with TOMS as a spokesperson for their gun control advocacy campaign.

---

45   Xue (2020)

Support those on the ground. This can mean several things. You can bring along a cooler of bottled water and pass it out to protestors or support organizations like Black Lives Matter by volunteering to help during the organizational/setup phase of a protest when it's less busy.

Do a survey about the issue and share the results. Get out your clipboard and join your child in asking people on the street for their opinion about important social justice matters like anti-racist activity. Share the results on social media. Even if it doesn't make a huge difference, your child will learn about opinion polling and may gain some insight into what other people think of issues that matter to them.

Raise/Donate money: Jonah Larsen is a twelve-year-old crochet artist from LaCrosse, Wisconsin who raises money for Ethiopian and local community charities with his craft work. He's written two books about crochet and has raised enough money to build a library in Ethiopia. He also runs his own LLC, Jonah's Hands, Inc.

Write a letter to a company: Kennedy Mitchum became frustrated that Merriam-Webster's definition of "racism" didn't include an entry for systemic racism and wrote the company asking that they change the definition. After reading her letter, Merriam-Webster updated their dictionary entry for racism.[46]

Call out the behavior of racists: After Mei-Ling Ho-Shing[47] survived the Parkland school shooting, she noticed her white classmates were getting most of the media attention and that students of color were under-represented in media accounts. She spoke up and the media started listening. Ho-Shing writes: "Gun violence is capable of affecting everyone. The movement needs to look like everyone."

---

46 Mosley (2020)
47 Nardino (2019)

Engage in community service. Join a civic organization like the Lion's Club and engage in community service with your kids. It will be a fun family activity that makes a difference.

Get the press involved: Thandiwe Abdullah wrote a scathing op-ed that went viral about media responses to the Parkland shooting and called for more intersectionality in the debate over gun control. She also organized within her community and among her classmates and has become a member of the Black Lives Matter LA Youth Vanguard.

Practice self-care: Felicia Fitzpatrick writes about self-care: "I consider it a form of activism."[48] Remember that it's okay to take a social media break or turn off the news and get into a bubble bath if it's too much for you to engage in activism at the moment. We all need to take a break. Teach your kids that it's okay to take care of themselves too. Self-care can also mean standing up against racism or for a cause that matters to your child. It will give them a place to channel their energy toward a good cause. Self-care sometimes means breaking toxic relationships that make us feel unsafe, physically and/ or emotionally, including distancing yourself from "friends" with anti-Blackness rhetoric. Do not hesitate to relieve yourself (and your child) of the anxiety and harm that other people's propaganda might be causing you.

Be joyful and hopeful: Darius Weems had never left his hometown of Athens, Georgia due to his Duchennes muscular dystrophy.[49] But he teamed up with several grassroots organizations to help him raise money and awareness and headed to Los Angeles with the hopes of having his wheelchair revamped on MTV's show *Pimp My Ride*. His journey was documented in the film *Darius Goes West* which raised awareness about the need for handicapped and wheelchair accessibility across the country.

---

48   Fitzpatrick (2017)
49   Steiger (2011)

Support marginalized-owned businesses: There are plenty of opportunities to support Black-owned businesses in your local area, but pay attention to young Black entrepreneurs who are starting up businesses, such as Mikayla Ulmer who pitched her business on *Shark Tank* at just nine years old. By the time she'd reached thirteen, she'd signed a deal with Whole Foods to carry her product BeeSweet Lemonade nationally.[50] Supporting young Black entrepreneurs teaches your kid the power of money and how they can direct it to causes they care about.

Create: Black, trans, independent filmmaker Fatima Jamal was disheartened by reading, "no fats, no femmes" on LGBTQ dating sites and set out to make a documentary, *No Fats, No Femmes* which she completed. She was named one of the coolest queers on the internet by *Teen Vogue.*[51]

Find what works for you: Thirteen-year-old Bishop Curry had an idea for a product that could save lives of children endangered by hot car deaths, but he didn't have the money to develop the prototype and bring it to market. He managed to raise $45,000 on his Go Fund Me page, built his prototype, filed for a patent, and is now producing his product called "Oasis."

How to Recognize Allies

Historically, Black people have done the most work and have borne the burden of making civil rights matters of national importance. However, white people still hold the majority of power within systemic racist societies like the United States and play an important role in attitude shifts and legislative changes. It is important for your child to learn what an ally is, and how to lean on them for support.

---

50 Bethea (2019)
51 Wicker (2019)

(By the way, there is a school of thought out there about allyship being bogus. Some Black activists believe there is no such thing as an ally. I personally believe in allyship.)

Here are some ways to recognize an ally:[52]

1. **They know racism can be everywhere, every day.** An ally recognizes even the microaggressions Black people deal with and speak up against them when they see them happening. They don't belittle Black people for being offended at racist behavior, no matter how minor it might seem to some. Allies understand that microaggressions can be just as harmful as overt racism.

2. **They notice how racism is denied, minimized, and justified.** Allies recognize when others try to minimize racist incidents or blame the victim of a racist encounter. They know that saying things like, "If he hadn't resisted arrest" are counterproductive and short-sighted. Groups like White Nonsense Roundup will actively push back against racism to prevent their Black allies from becoming mentally exhausted.

3. **They understand and learn from the history of whiteness and racism.** An ally might not know all the history of racism in the United States (that is something many Black people are also still learning), but they are willing to listen and learn as much as they can about the role white privilege has played in inequality.

4. **They understand the connections between racism, economic issues, sexism, and other forms of injustice.** Allies understand that racism is a complex issue and that the impact of racism is broad-based and affects women and those with limited incomes disproportionately. They recognize the role racism plays in other kinds of injustice.

---

52   "Checklist for While Allies Against Racism" (2020); Kiver (n.d); Pruitt (2015)

5. **They take a stand against injustice.** Allies speak up for—not over—people of color. If they see an injustice occurring, they will make noise, but allow a person of color to advocate for themselves. They know how to be supportive without usurping anyone's right to stand up for themselves.

6. **They don't call names and they're not personally abusive.** Allies don't toss around racist slang to sound cool, and they aren't abusive to anyone of any color.

7. **They support the leadership of people of color.** Allies vote and campaign for the people they believe are the best candidates, regardless of color, and they are critical of any leader who is deserving of scrutiny. They are comfortable taking a subordinate role to a Black supervisor or having a Black boss at their job.

8. **They have conversations about whiteness in white spaces.** An ally will bring up white privilege to those who are using it to limit others. They aren't afraid of being ostracized or criticized for taking a stand against racism wherever it occurs.

9. **They don't settle for being enlightened.** It's not enough for an ally to understand racism. They actively seek out ways to support people of color in their struggle.

10. **They listen to experiences outside of their racial reality, and they believe them.** Allies are willing to listen and believe people of color when they describe racist incidents. They don't argue about whether or not an action was racist or make excuses for the perpetrator. They are open-minded.

11. **They recognize the limitations of white people in working toward racial justice.** An ally understands that they are there to *help* with individual battles, not fight the whole war themselves. They stand down for people of color and let them lead the fight while simultaneously lending support.

12. **They ensure the inclusion of people of color in group settings.** Allies work to diversify workplaces and other group events like committee meetings.

13. **They continuously raise issues about racism in public and in private.** They point out racism when they see it happening and educate their children about racism.

14. **They set high expectations for people of color.** Allies expect the people they support to stretch beyond what they think they are capable of achieving, and support people of color in their endeavors, no matter how big they may be. Not so long ago, the idea of a Black man in the White House was unheard of. Allies helped get Barack Obama elected, and when he won the presidential election, they helped to ensure he kept working to build a better country for everyone.

15. **They take a personal interest in the lives of individuals.** Allies befriend people of color and care genuinely about them. They don't speak in terms of "us" and "them."

In this excerpt of Brian Crooks' story, he discusses how he discovered a friend was not a true ally:

I went to the University of Iowa, which is a very white campus in a very white state. It's funny, because most of the people I met there who came from small-town Iowa were really excited to finally meet a Black person. And it wasn't like they wanted me to be a mascot; they genuinely wanted a Black friend so they could learn about Black people and stuff. It was nice. On the other hand, if I was in a bar and talking to a girl they didn't think I should be talking to, or in their drunken state they bumped into sober me, you'd be surprised to see how quickly some of these guys will call a complete stranger a nigger. (...)

One summer when I was back from college, I had an argument with a good friend of mine. When I say "good friend," I mean that this is a guy I knew since middle school. Our dads used to work together.

I can't count how many times I had spent the night at his parents' house. But we had an argument. The kind of argument most friends have at one point or another. This time, he decided to get really, really racial about it. He started off by telling me I should be ashamed of my complexion (he later claimed that he meant I had bad skin; only I'd only had like two pimples in my entire life). Then, he said I belonged in the ghetto, not Naperville. In the end, he looked me dead in the face and called me a nigger. Again, this was one of my closest friends.

Since then, I've completely cut him out of my life. But it fits with the experiences that I've had too many times; people can be totally cool for years and years but suddenly decide that they need to be super racist because they want to hurt you. They'll say they're sorry, they'll explain how you misinterpreted what they said, but the fact is, they reach for racism because they think it'll emotionally and psychologically destroy you, and that's what they want to do at that moment.

A Note on Performative Allyship

Performative allyship needs to be recognized and called out when it occurs. A performative ally is one who "talks the talk" but doesn't "walk the walk."

Kristina Gill, the coauthor of *Tasting Rome*, gives an example of her experience with performative allyship as it pertains to the publication of her book. On Instagram she detailed how the publisher of her book left her out of editorial decisions and left all of the decisions up to her white coauthor. She wasn't even listed as a coauthor on the book, even though she had written much of the text. Gill was left out of the foreword notes, and in the post-publication publicity tour wasn't invited to appear at events publicizing the book, while her white coauthor was booked for signings at bookstores and for media events. Gill's contribution to the book was limited to a photography credit, and even that wasn't respected in many of the post-publication press releases, where all of the credit was given to her white coauthor. Gill's own agent didn't stand up for her during the publication process, and later issued an apology for not making sure Gill got the credit she deserved. And several months after the book was published, Gill's coauthor was given a second book contract without submitting a proposal, while Gill heard nothing at all.

In June of 2020, in an unrelated issue, several editors at *Bon Appétit* magazine resigned after it was revealed there was a pervasive culture of racism in the magazine's hierarchy, including photos of one of the editors in brownface.

Some signs of performative allyship:

1. **White fragility:** When confronted with a racist action, the performative ally becomes defensive.

2. **Virtue signaling:** Making public statements that reinforce the idea that the performative ally was acting in the best interests of the person wronged.

3. **Self-centering:** The performative ally focuses the situation on themselves and ignores the harm done to the person of color.

4. **Faux Ally benefits:** The person who benefits from the collaboration with a person of color is the performative ally, usually to the detriment of the person of color.

5. **Statements appear after being called out:** We see this all the time, especially with the #MeToo movement, where carefully prepared PR statements and apologies are sent out, but very little actually changes.

6. **Band wagoning:** The performative ally moves quickly to gain support, often belittling or blaming the person of color that was wronged.

7. **PR/Brand/Public image management:** In a situation like Kristina Gill's where the incident was made public, and there

were publicists involved, a concerted effort to remake the performative ally's image may occur.

A genuine ally knows that racism hurts everyone trapped in the system. They don't look for credit or accolades. They look for and work toward real, lasting change, and they are willing to give credit where credit is due. Encourage your children to find their own allies by pointing out your allies to them.

Chapter 6

Racial Profiling and Police Encounters

Darren Martin, a former White House Staffer under President Obama, just wanted to move into his new home. While in the process of doing just that, he found himself surrounded by half a dozen New York City policemen who were under the impression he might be armed and dangerous. One of his new neighbors had seen him moving in, and assumed he was an armed burglar. "It could have been the TV, the couch, the pillows—I don't know," Martin said. "It's a fear of Black men that makes people see things."[53]

The problem of racial profiling is one that impacts many people of color. Even non-Blacks. And it's a much broader issue than just increased police calls for suspicious activity. Think of a post 9/11 world, where travelers of Middle Eastern descent are subject to "no fly" lists and more thorough TSA screening at airports or of anti-immigrant sentiments that lead to increased immigration raids in areas with high Latinx populations.

Blacks, Asians and Hispanics are all typically subject to higher interest rates on car loans, even if they have the same credit score as a white customer. In job interviews, Black candidates are likely to have their interviews cut short by 25 percent over their white counterparts,

53   Yan (2018)

and resumes with stereotypical Black names receive 50 percent less callbacks than those with stereotypical white names. Studies show that Black women with natural hairstyles are less likely to get a call for a job interview.

The phrase coined to describe this kind of behavior is "implicit bias" and it has a broad ripple effect. It starts with preconceptions developed during childhood and ends with more police calls and arrests for Black and other minority citizens than for whites. Racial profiling in law enforcement isn't good for anyone. It bogs down police departments with unnecessary calls and can create a schism between police and the communities they are sworn to serve and protect.

Police Encounters

The statistics for Black people and law enforcement are alarming when placed in comparison to those of white people. Black people are subject to more traffic stops.[54] They are 3.5 times more likely than whites to be shot and killed when unarmed.[55] They are more likely to be handcuffed and detained without arrest, pepper sprayed or pushed to the ground compared to whites, and four times more likely than whites to be searched.

In Falcon Heights, Minnesota, where Philando Castile was shot and killed during a routine traffic stop for a broken taillight, Black people make up only 7 percent of the population, but constituted 47 percent of the arrests that year. It's important to prepare your child for the likelihood they will be stopped by police, because no matter how law-abiding they are, there's a good chance they'll have to cope with the police at some point.

---

54 CNN Library (2020)
55 Weir (2016)

Rules may vary from one state to another, but there are generally three types of typical police encounters:[56]

Consensual Encounter

During this kind of police encounter, the officer initiates a conversation that doesn't involve any show of force like police sirens or orders. The civilian is free to leave and has the right not to answer any questions or identify themselves.

Investigatory Detention

During this kind of stop, there is reasonable suspicion of criminal activity. The person being detained must identify themselves. You do have a Fifth Amendment right to remain silent during an investigatory stop.

The officer stopping you usually has the right to perform a brief frisk for weapons (check the rules for your state), and if one is located, may perform a full search. You still have the right to refuse a full search, but the officer may do this against your will (again, check the rules as they apply to your state). You do not have the right to walk away during an investigatory stop. Probable cause that a crime has been or is about to be committed must exist for an investigatory stop to take place.

Arrest

In order for an arrest to occur, there must be probable cause to believe you have committed a crime. In an arrest, physical force or authority is used to prevent you from leaving, and typically a person is placed

---

56   "What You Need to Know about Police Encounters" (n.d).

in handcuffs. You have your Fifth Amendment right to remain silent during an arrest, but must cooperate with the police. You do not have the right to leave.

Your Rights during a Police Encounter

Please check whether these apply to your state, but these are your common rights:

You have the right to remain silent. You may be required to identify yourself, but have the right to indicate you do not wish to speak with the police or answer any questions (Google "Miranda Rights"). You do not have to answer any questions about where you were born, how you entered the country or your immigration status in most police encounters, though this may be different in an airport or at a border crossing.

You have the right to an attorney. You can refuse to answer any questions without legal counsel. You may have the right to have an attorney provided for you if you are arrested and cannot afford an attorney.[57]

You have the right to refuse to be searched. A police officer can pat you down for weapons, and may conduct a search without your consent, but it will be noted if the search was consensual or not.

Know your rights![58] "Teaching your children what they have the right to say—and not say—during a traffic stop can be key, says lawyer Patrice James. James is a former public defender and now works as the director of community justice at the Shriver Center on Poverty Law. She says it's fine for kids to give their names to an officer, but

---

57   "Stopped by Police" (2019)

58   Ali (2020)

once the questions go beyond that, they should immediately ask for two things: a parent and a lawyer."[59]

A portion of Brian Crooks' story on Facebook relates a harrowing police encounter just up the street from his parents' home in Naperville, Illinois.

Once, when Brian Crooks went home on a visit from college, he was pulled over less than a block from his parents' home. It was a late winter night, around midnight, and it had snowed that day, so Brian wasn't speeding. He hadn't been drinking either. The police officer had his gun drawn when he stepped out of the cruiser. He told Brian to drop his keys out the window, and to exit his car with his hands up and step backward toward him slowly. Brian knew the police officer was off base, but he also knew that any failure to comply might be interpreted as an act of aggression. He didn't want to be shot to death—particularly not down the street from his parents' house. So he did as he was told.

The policeman handcuffed and frisked him, and Brian spent about fifteen minutes handcuffed in the cold while the officer searched his car. The officer refused to explain why Brian had been pulled over, or why he was being detained. It was only when Brian was secured in the back of the squad car that the officer explained there had been reports of gang activity in the area, and that a car and driver that matched his description was involved in said gang activity. Gang activity in south Naperville didn't sound likely—and neither did the idea that it was committed by a Black male driving a flashy blue Mazda MX-6 with a showy blue and white interior.

The policeman was very short when he asked what Brian was doing in that neighborhood so late at night. When Brian explained that his parents lived at "the house with the glass basketball backboard just over there," the policeman didn't believe him. He had Brian exit the squad car once again and placed him face down on the hood to frisk him one more time. Brian's identification listed his parents' address, but the policeman still didn't believe that he lived in that house. Brian thought the policeman might accuse him of having a fake license. It was only after about a half hour when his record was cleared, his car was searched for the third time, and nothing was found that the policeman let Brian go reluctantly.

The policeman didn't apologize, or admit his mistake, and of course he wouldn't acknowledge that he'd lied about a Black gang leader in south Naperville driving a gaudy blue Mazda MX-6. The officer watched from his squad car as Brian drove to his parents' house and stayed outside in the street as Brian opened the garage door, parked his car inside, and then shut the garage door.

When Police Encounters Turn Deadly

Over the past thirty years, a number of police encounters have made national headlines and led to civic unrest as protests and riots erupted in their wake.[60] In many instances, these police encounters turned deadly. Unfortunately, many people downplay the problem.

The Statistical Paradox of Police Killings

Some people are quick to argue that Blacks are more likely to be killed than whites in a police encounter due to the number of encounters and increased crime rates among Black citizens. However, Blacks only make up 37 percent of the population. The increase in deaths can also be attributed to increased police encounters due to implicit bias and racial profiling. Whites are less likely to have an encounter with the

---

60   Ross (2015)

police unless the situation is dire. Blacks get stopped for mundane issues more often.[61]

What About "Black-on-Black Crime"?

Black-on-black crime is a racist trope. While Blacks kill Blacks at higher rates than whites kill Blacks—whites also are more likely to kill whites.[62] Let's call it what it is: crime by proximity. Educate yourself. Please look up real statistics in order to debunk the myth of "Black-on-black crime."[63]

What About "Black-on-White Crime"?

This idea, that Blacks are hunting down and raping or killing white people, is rooted in white conspiracy theory. The rate at which whites die from Black-perpetrated crime is about 15 percent according to the FBI. In some false reports, it has been reported to be as high as 82 percent. It's just a flat-out lie.[64]

Some Interesting Facts

Here are some interesting facts from Pew Research Center:[65]

- **Blacks and whites overwhelmingly agree that the police and the criminal justice system treats Blacks unfairly.** 84 percent of Blacks and 63 percent of whites agree that police treat Blacks

---

61   Clayton (2020)
62   Smith (2020)
63   Coates (2014); Massie (2016); Smith (2020)
64   "The Biggest Lie in the White Supremacist Propaganda Playbook: Unraveling the Truth About 'Black-on-White Crime" (2018)
65   Desilver (2020)

unfairly, while 87 percent of Blacks and 61 percent of whites say the same about the criminal justice system.

- **Blacks are five times more likely than whites to say they have been stopped unfairly by police.** 44 percent of Blacks say this, while only 9 percent of whites say they have been stopped unfairly, and Black men are more likely than Black women to say they have been stopped unreasonably, 59 percent of Black men vs. 31 percent Black women.

- **65 percent of Blacks say they have been treated unfairly or suspiciously because of their race or ethnicity,** while only 24 percent of whites say they have been treated suspiciously because of race or ethnicity.

- **In a 2016 survey, only 33 percent of Blacks thought police did a good job of policing** in terms of using the right amount of force, treating ethnic groups fairly, or holding officers accountable for misconduct.

- **68 percent of police said Black Lives Matter demonstrations were due to anti-police bias.** Only 10 percent felt that demonstrations were an attempt to have police held accountable for misconduct.

How to Stay Safe During a Police Encounter

- Remain calm.
- Keep your hands visible at all times.
- Be polite and cooperative, but do protect your rights.
- Don't run, resist or obstruct the police.
- Don't lie or provide false documentation.
- Keep your vehicle in good operating condition.
- Make sure you have your paperwork handy.

- Don't argue with the police.

- Turn off the ignition in your vehicle.

- Explain where your paperwork is before reaching for it.

- Ask the officer to turn on his body camera.

- If you feel unsafe, call 911 and ask the dispatcher to send a Sergeant or Lieutenant to assist you.

Living while Black

The sad truth is that being Black by itself is reason enough to expect that the police will be called. Black people are subject to having the police called on them for all manner of everyday, mundane activities like waiting for a business associate in a Starbucks and asking to use the restroom, babysitting non-Black children, having a backyard barbecue, not waving to a neighbor while leaving an Airbnb or shopping while pregnant.[66] Henry Louis Gates Jr. was arrested for "breaking into his own home" in Cambridge, Massachusetts near Harvard University's campus.[67]

The prevalence of these types of stories has led to the founding of an advocacy organization called Living While Black that tracks and reports on instances where Black people going about their everyday routine find themselves handcuffed or questioned by police because someone found their mere presence suspicious.[68] The number of stories from ordinary law-abiding Black people who've been suspected of criminal activity due to racial profiling is staggering.

There is no one good reason for this to happen, but some of the causes of unwarranted police calls have to do with how we live in

---

66   Griggs (2018)
67   Goodnough (2009)
68   Lockhart (2018)

the United States. Despite the repeal of Jim Crow laws, the US is still largely segregated by community and many white people have little to no contact with Black people in the course of their ordinary days; so simply seeing a Black person in a place where they are not accustomed to seeing them can send up a red flag. This is not to say that anyone's freedom to move should be limited in order to pacify anyone else's fears, but you and your children should be aware of the phenomenon so you can be prepared to react in a way that will minimize the chances of a civilian or police encounter escalating to arrest or violence.

And this unwarranted harassment starts early, so it's important that your child understands that as innocent as their actions may be, the color of their skin is enough to trigger a defensive reaction in some people, and they may find themselves facing a squad of police officers or an angry mob just because of their race.

"The Talk," by Age

There have been no studies yet that conclude how people of different races should talk to their kids about what to do if stopped by the police, but experts agree that all kids, no matter the race, need to be prepared to deal with the police starting when they go to school (and are likely to start having police encounters).[69] Here are some guidelines that may help.

Elementary School (starting at about five years old)

Give details about what's going on in the media about policing, but don't use terminology your child doesn't yet understand. Teach your child that the police are meant to serve and protect them, but that

---

sometimes things go wrong and people get hurt. Teach them to treat police with respect. Tell them that if they are stopped by the police, they should ask for their parents.

Read *Something Happened in Our Town* by Marianne Celano, Marietta Collins, and Ann Hazzard. This book shows the reactions of two families, one white and one black, after a black man is shot by a police officer in their town. Josh and Emma know that something bad has happened in their town, and they have lots of questions about it: *Why did the police officer shoot the man? Why are people upset about it? Can a police officer be arrested?*

Young Adolescents | Tweens (starting at about ten to twelve years old)

At this age, you can start talking to your child about concepts like police brutality, discrimination, and racial injustice. Use historical examples, or examples from the media. Explain inequality in the justice system in an age-appropriate manner. Let them know that more Black people are arrested, and more Black people are imprisoned, and that it's not always fair.

I suggest reading *Ghost Boys* by Jewell Parker Rhodes. In the story, Jerome is a young boy who is shot by a police officer while playing with a toy gun. As a ghost, he sees the effects of his death on his family, friends, and community. He encounters the ghost of Emmett Till, and connects in the living world with the daughter of the police officer that shot him. This powerful novel is an important read for kids ages eight and up.

Another good book is *The Hate U Give* by Angie Thomas, in which the main character Starr feels caught between two worlds: the black world of her neighborhood Garden Heights, and the white world of the private school she attends. School Starr and Home Starr are two vastly different people. It's a good choice for both tweens and teens.

Teenagers (thirteen and up)

Explain implicit bias to your child and how it may affect them if stopped by the police. Make sure they understand that adultification may lead the police to treat them as if they are much older and possibly more aggressive than they appear to be. Share research with them. Teach your children about the different kinds of police stops and their rights. Tell them they should be polite, but avoid answering questions other than identity without a lawyer or parent present.

Continue using literature as conversation-starters with your child. In the book *All American Boys* by Jason Reynolds and Brendan Kiely, Rashad's life is changed when a simple trip to purchase a bag of chips leads to him being beaten by a police officer who thinks he's shoplifting. What happens afterward polarizes his school and eventually the nation.

In May 2018, Marcus-David Peters, a high school biology teacher who moonlighted as a part-time security guard at a hotel, had a psychiatric episode and left his second job unclothed. After he veered off a highway in Richmond, Virginia and crashed his car, he was approached by police officer Michael Nyantaki, who tried to subdue him with a Taser. When that failed, Nyantaki shot two bullets into Peters' stomach, killing him. Peters had no criminal history, and no prior history of psychiatric episodes.

This killing highlights the many problems Black people with a disability or a mental illness face in the United States. Studies show that the number of people with disabilities and/or mental illness make up 1/3 to ½ of all police killings.[70]

70 Abrams (2020)

Black people with a disability and/or mental illness are especially at risk of being killed by police:

- Black people are more likely to have chronic health issues.

- Black people are less likely to be formally diagnosed with disabilities and/or mental illness due to many socioeconomic factors like lower incomes.

- They are three times as likely as whites to be killed by police.

- Complicating this is the "compliance culture" of policing. If someone doesn't respond to a police order to halt, the police are likely to move in with force. Some people, like those in the deaf community, may not hear the order. Others may not understand the command.

- On average, police receive just eight hours of crisis/de-escalation training, compared to an average of fifty-eight hours of firearm training.

- Some jurisdictions are moving toward a new model of policing where, instead of an armed police response to calls for psychiatric episodes, a crisis team of mental health workers responds. This has shown promising results in pilot programs around the country.

Is it time to shift focus?

Many critics are saying that the Talk isn't effective.[71] It may be true that no matter how well you prepare your child for a police encounter, things can go wrong, and no amount of preparation can protect them from a trigger-happy police officer. Some police are just bad. And yes, the focus should shift toward holding rogue police officers accountable for acts of brutality, but this doesn't have to be a "one or the other" proposition. We can all work toward racial justice while still preparing our kids for the chance that they will have to deal

---

71   Blake (2020); Hart (2017)

with the police at some point in their lives.[72] Even if police reform does go through, children should still know their rights and what to do if questioned by the police. It may not help in every situation, but in the majority of police encounters, knowing how to behave can help save your child's life and preserve their civil rights.

72   Belk (2019)

Chapter 7

How to Explain Systemic Racism to Your Child

Many people argue that we live in a post-racial society in the United States, and that racism ended when Jim Crow laws were repealed and the Civil Rights Act passed Congress. But this is simplistic thinking. Racism is still alive and thriving today in America and around the globe, and you'll have to explain to your child that the American government has discriminatory policies set up based on the disturbing idea that white people are better or smarter than Black people.[73]

For a brief primer on systemic racism that you can watch with your teen, check out Racism is Real (www.youtube.com/watch?time_continue=2&v=fTcSVQJ2h8g), which provides a quick explanation of systemic racism. Then ask these questions: How did this video change your opinions on racism? In what ways can non-Black people gain advantages from racism even if they aren't trying to take advantage of the system? Which advantages did you see non-Black people getting from systemic racism in the video?

---

73 "On Views of Race and Inequality, Blacks and Whites Are Worlds Apart" (2016)

What exactly is systemic racism?

In short, it's a political system that adheres to policies designed to discriminate against one or more races of people. This discrimination can take many forms, but we typically think of it in terms of equal access, opportunity, and justice; it has become so embedded in our society, that it's often hard to recognize as part of a system designed to make life more difficult for Black people.[74]

It was not always so subtle. One of the delegates at the Mississippi constitutional convention of 1890 put it bluntly: "It is the manifest intention of this convention to secure to the State of Mississippi, 'white supremacy.' "[75] That kind of language in a state house would be unacceptable today, but that doesn't mean the problem has gone away. It's just gone underground.

In their 1967 book, *Black Power: The Politics of Liberation*, Stokely Carmichael and Charles V. Hamilton wrote about systemic racism:[76]

> "When a black family moves into a home in a white neighborhood and is stoned, burned or routed out, they are victims of an overt act of individual racism which most people will condemn. But it is institutional racism that keeps black people locked in dilapidated slum tenements, subject to the daily prey of exploitative slumlords, merchants, loan sharks and discriminatory real estate agents. The society either pretends it does not know of this latter situation or is in fact incapable of doing anything meaningful about it."

Systemic racism is an insidious part of the fabric of our lives, and the mechanism by which it is woven into our daily consciousness is similar to how we create habits. You can think of it in much the same way a person develops a fitness routine. Say you want to start

---

74 "What Is Systemic Racism?" (n.d.)

75 Blow (2020)

76 O'Dowd (2020)

a daily practice of running. For the first couple of weeks, it's difficult
to get up in the morning, lace up your running shoes, and get out for
a jog. Maybe you huff and puff and struggle to meet your goal; your
running shoes aren't broken in at the beginning, and you find yourself
sore and blistered at the end of the run, but over time, it becomes just
another part of your daily routine; your body adjusts to the exercise.
Your shoes get broken in, and you hardly feel the pain you felt at the
beginning. Your feet develop calluses to protect you from the chafing
your feet took in the beginning.

Systemic racism is like that. In the beginning, when it was being
established, it was more overt than it is today. People were very direct
about their intent to enslave thousands of Africans in the United
States, but over time, it became just another part of the daily routine
of life in the United States. To be clear, systemic racism is not the kind
of overt racism you see in hooded Ku Klux Klan members or white
supremacists; it's much sneakier than that, and not always easy to
recognize. Throughout this chapter, we'll look at how systemic racism
affects Black people in a variety of different ways and share more of
Brian Crooks's story as it relates to both overt and systemic racism,
to illustrate how vigilant you must be to recognize the more systemic
brand of racism.

Children and Racism

We've gone over how children are affected by racism in other
chapters, but some of this bears repeating. Children are affected
by systemic racism in a myriad of ways. Here are some of the most
important facts for you to keep in mind with your own children:

- Black children make up about 18 percent of the preschool
  population but are given out of school suspension about 50
  percent of the time.

- In K–12 schools, Black kids are three times as likely to be suspended as whites. Black girls are even more at a disadvantage as they are seen as combative and angry, and not pretty enough to be included as part of other groups.
- 40 percent of school expulsions are Black children.
- 2/3 of student disturbances forwarded to the police to handle are Black or Hispanic children.
- 1/5 of students with disabilities are Black, but they are placed in mechanical restraints 44 percent of the time and are placed in seclusion 42 percent of the time. Black children are eighteen times as likely as white children to be sentenced as adults. 60 percent of the child population in prison are Black children.
- Black college graduates are two times as likely as white graduates to have trouble finding a job after graduation.

Income Inequality

One of the most obvious ways systemic racism affects Black people is in how it translates into the bottom line.[77] When Black people are valued less than their white counterparts, as a result, we tend to be worth less money.

- The jobless rate for Blacks is two times that of the jobless rate for whites.
- For every $10,000 in salary increase, the chances of a Black person losing their job increases by 7 percent.
- 73 percent of whites own homes compared to 43 percent of Blacks.
- The white median household income is $91,000. The median household income for Black is just $7,000.

---

77   Collins (2020)

- Homes in Black neighborhoods are priced 23 percent lower than homes in white neighborhoods. This amounts to about $156 billion in lost revenue.[78]

Criminal Justice System

The United States has the highest per capita prison population in the world, and it should come as no surprise that a large percentage of the imprisoned population in the United States is made up of Black prisoners who are incarcerated at much higher percentages than any other race.[79]

- Blacks are three times as likely to be searched at a traffic stop and six times as likely to go to jail.

- Black people make up 13 percent of the total population in the US and 14 percent of people who use drugs monthly, but comprise 37 percent of the people arrested for drug offenses.

- Black convicts make up 56 percent of the people serving prison sentences for drug offenses.

- In New York City, Black people make up 50 percent of the population, but are stopped by NYPD 80 percent of the time they make a stop. Once stopped, only 8 percent of white people are frisked, while Blacks and Latinx are frisked 85 percent of the time they are stopped.

- A Black person convicted of killing a white person is twice as likely to receive the death penalty as a white person convicted of killing a Black person.

- A Black person is more likely to see his charge upgraded to a felony murder offense.

78   Perry (2020)
79   Carson 2015; Nesbit 2015; "How to end institutional racism" (2016)

- Once arrested, Black people spend longer times in jail awaiting trial. A Black person is 33 percent more likely to wait in jail for a felony offense than a white person.

- 2/3 of the people serving life sentences are Black prisoners.

- Potential Black jurors are dismissed 80 percent of the time.

- ¼ of death penalty cases have no Black jurors.

- Black people serve, on average, about 20 percent longer prison sentences.

- 77 percent of death row inmates killed a white person. Only 13 percent are there because they killed a Black person.

- One out of every three Black men can expect to go to prison in their lifetimes.[80]

- Black women are three times as likely as white women to be incarcerated.

- 13 percent of Black men in the United States are ineligible to vote because of felony disenfranchisement.

- Once released from prison, only 5 percent of Black felons receive a callback on a job application compared to white felons. White criminals actually have better callback rates for jobs than Black people with no criminal history.[81]

Health

Aside from the strain that the daily stress of systemic racism places on the Black body, which is to a large extent immeasurable on an individual level, there are some measurable ways in which the health of Black people is impacted by our system of racism.[82]

---

80   Kerby (2012)
81   Quigley (2010)
82   Young (2020); "How to end institutional racism" (2016)

- Before the Affordable Care Act (ACA) passed, one in five Black Americans was insured. Since it was passed into law, the rates of uninsured have dropped across all racial groups, but there are still 30,000,000 people uninsured. About half of that number are people of color.

- Fourteen states have refused to expand Medicaid under the ACA, including states that have the highest population of Black Americans.

- White babies die before their first birthday at a rate of about 4.9 per 1,000. White mothers die from pregnancy or childbirth complications at about 13 per 100,000. Compare that to Black babies, who die before their first birthday at a rate of about 11.4 per 1,000, and Black mothers, who die from pregnancy or childbirth complications at about 42.8 per 100,000 mothers. "A growing body of research suggests that stress related to the day-in, day-out experience of racism may be a key factor contributing to the infant mortality rate."[83]

Black people are shaped and affected by systemic racism, starting from a very young age through adulthood. The weariness is palpable. But what can be done to fight systemic racism when the people fighting it are worn out?

Never argue with an idiot

Here is the message you should convey to your child:

No matter how vocal and active you are, there are just some people who will never accept that systemic racism and implicit bias are issues in this day and age. You can run yourself ragged trying to convince a bigot that he or she is bigoted, and the only thing that will accomplish is that you'll wear yourself out fighting a losing battle. It's not your job

---

83 "Bearing the Burden: How Racism-Related Stress Hurts America's Black Mothers and Babies" (n.d.).

to convince the world that Black Lives Matter. Some people cannot be swayed no matter how persuasive the arguments you provide them.

Rather than providing racists with research, point them in the right direction, and let them research the issue themselves. If they aren't willing to put in the legwork to educate themselves, they simply aren't interested in learning. There is only so much you can do with people who are willfully ignorant.

Do answer questions. People are capable of change, but they need to show a willingness to learn. It may be awkward for them at first. Be patient, but suggest they talk to other people of color so you aren't alone in trying to sway someone. A person is more likely to see the other side if they have more than one resource to rely on. Suggest that they step out of their comfort zone and just listen to what is being said.

But put your energy toward community alliances and group efforts. It's okay not to win every debate.

How to Fight Systemic Racism

- **Test yourself!** I suggested earlier in this book taking one of the implicit bias tests created by a consortium of scholars at the University of Washington, Harvard University, and the University of Virginia. These tests (there are several) measure your unconscious bias toward other people of different races, ethnicities and religions. You may discover that you have some hidden biases of your own to be mindful of. The tests can be found at implicit.harvard.edu/implicit/takeatest.html.

  Encourage your child to take the test as well and discuss the results together.

- **Speak up!** If you see (or are the victim of) overt racism and it is safe to do so, say something. Challenge racist behavior.

Encourage your child to speak up as well (but, again, only when it's safe for them to do so).

- **Defend democracy.** Attend protests and town hall meetings where racism is a central concern. If you can afford to, support local and regional bail bond funds that help provide legal assistance to demonstrators who are arrested while exercising their civil rights.[84]

- **Learn anti-Black history.** There are a number of documentaries and podcasts available for you to watch and listen to, including Ava DuVernay's documentary *13th*, available on Netflix. Or listen and read *The 1619 Project*, available on the web. (The project has become controversial, and the controversy itself is quite fascinating.) Knowing about the early days of systemic racism in the country will help you (and your child) put in context what is happening today.

- **Know your rights.** And defend them. Check out the ACLU, the Southern Poverty Law Center, and other organizations that work to protect civil liberties. Demand action by contacting your local leaders, but don't stop there. Contact your representatives in Congress and the Senate. Sign petitions. Vote with your conscience.

- **Challenge the notion of color-blindness.** Color-blindness actually makes racism worse, because it rests on the supposition that all races are treated equally. While it may be true that we *are* all equal, we are not *treated* equally, and color-blindness just creates an excuse for people to overlook inequity when it's apparent.

- **Find out if your work or school district has programs to help minorities thrive.** If they don't exist, work to develop a program for mentorship.

---

84   "8 Everyday Ways to Fight Racism" (2017)

- **Put your money where your mouth is.** Join the boycott of companies that don't actively fight for equal justice. Spend your money at Black-owned businesses, and, if you can, support organizations that work to fight systemic racism.

Teach all of this to your children. The best way to fight systemic racism is by teaching the next generation about how pervasive and insidious it is.

Shocking Racist Traditions

Much of the information in this section should outrage and disturb you, and you should question what, if anything, you choose to share with your children. Knowing about the more disturbing aspects of our racist past is important for your kids to understand our racist present, but keep your child's age in mind. It may be that your child isn't ready to know this part of their history just yet. If you have high school aged children, understanding the magnitude of racism in the past may give them hope for a better future as many of these behaviors are simply unacceptable in today's world.

Some of the problems of the past still resurface from time to time; for example, just about every Halloween, someone makes the news for wearing blackface. Regardless of whether sharing this information is something you feel is right, understanding the magnitude of our past history will help you understand many of the prevalent attitudes that we still face every day in the world.

The African Dodger or "Hit the Nigger Baby"

For much of the nineteenth and early twentieth centuries, up until the mid-1940s, "hit the nigger baby" or "the African dodger" was a popular carnival game.[85] Typically, a player was given three balls for about a nickel and would throw them at a Black person who was supposed to dodge the flying balls. If the ball hit its target, a prize was awarded. It is no surprise that many of the Black people who took part in this game suffered serious injuries. It was reported in St. Louis in 1913 that carnival organizers were "unable for hours today to secure an 'African Dodger' who would allow baseballs to be thrown at his cranium at the usual rate of three for 5 cents;" rumors had gone out that Hall of Fame fastball pitcher Walter Johnson was at the fair.

An advertisement for an African Dodger in 1924 reads:

Wants African Dodger to Face Balls at Club Fair

Do you want to earn a few precious dollars on the evening of September 19 and 20?

If you do and if you are not at all particular as to what happens to your head why apply at Room 10 in the building at 144 Pine street. Ask for Charlie and tell him you "saw his ad in the paper." Charlie is looking for a lion-hearted and hard-headed young man who will act as an African dodger at the big carnival to be staged by the West Barrington Community Club. The reward? That is a little matter that you can adjust with Charlie. He will treat you fairly and will see that you reach the Rhode Island Hospital safely in the event that that [sic] one of the baseballs comes in contact with your head.

We beg your pardon for not detailing the duties of an African dodger. He just puts his head through a hole in a big piece of canvass and permits the aforesaid head to be used as a target by young men who toss baseballs.

---

85   "The African Dodger" (2012)

> One day last week an African dodger was killed in Elizabeth, NJ, and
> the week before a dodger was killed in Hackensack, but don't permit
> these deaths to influence you.

If you couldn't make it to the fair, there was an African dodger table
game available with a mechanical Black man's head poking out of
a tiny hole so that you could play the game in the comfort of your
own home. Black people have traditionally, in the United States and
elsewhere, been the object of entertainment, often at our expense.

The Minstrel Show

The minstrel show began to rise to popularity in the mid-nineteenth
century, and continued through the beginning of the early twentieth
century until it was replaced by vaudeville.[86] A central attraction of
the minstrel show were performers who appeared in blackface and
portrayed Blacks as lazy and buffoonish and dim-witted. There were a
couple of traveling minstrel shows that employed Black entertainers,
but the majority were comprised of white performers. A minstrel
show typically followed a three-act structure and included plantation
comedy, a pun-filled stump speech and slapstick performance.
Minstrel shows lost popularity as the civil rights movement gained
momentum, and were practically phased out by the mid-1950s,
though some high school reimaginings of blackfaced minstrel shows
were performed right up through the 1960s. Some blackface traditions
continue around the globe, even today.

---

86 "Blackface: The Sad History of Minstrel Shows" (2019)

Black Pete and Blackface Around the World

For the past several years, Christmas in the Netherlands has been accompanied by widespread protests over "Zware Piete" or Black Pete, Santa Claus's companion.[87] It is a tradition in Holland for people to dress in blackface, don large Afro wigs and speak in fake Caribbean accents as Santa Claus makes his appearance to herald in the year's yuletide festivities. The tradition of Black Pete comes from the mid-nineteenth century when he was seen as a mockery of the devil who'd come dressed in the disguise of a Black Moor. Black Pete is typically a comic foil for Santa Claus and is a stereotypical dim-witted buffoon who threatens to kidnap children who have behaved badly and beat them with a pole.

Black Pete is just one example of the caricature of blackface that continues to be seen around the world. At this point, we can view it as a racist archetype of the dim-witted, happy-go-lucky, musical athletic, on the plantation negro that rose to prominence under colonial rule and continues to resurface globally. The tradition of blackface can be traced back to the mid-fifteenth century when Portuguese explorers captured Africans and brought them home to display publicly. Other vestiges of racism continue to be recognized in our culture, suggesting how much work still has to be done to fight racism.

There is now discussion of doing away with the Black Pete tradition, but nothing has been executed yet.

Gator Bait

In June 2020, the University of Florida announced plans to end its "gator bait" football chant over protests that the cheer brought to

---

mind the racist tradition of using Black Americans as gator bait. The university president stated he had no idea that the chant might be connected to a dark history, but a little bit of research shows it was a horrific example of how Blacks have been abused historically.

Black Babies and Alligators

- A June 3, 1908 *Washington Times* headline reads "Baits Alligators with Pickaninnies." The article continues, "Zoo Specimens Coaxed to Summer Quarters by Plump Little Africans." According to the article, the New York Zoological Gardens' zookeeper sent two black children into an enclosure housing more than twenty-five crocodiles and alligators. The children then fled, leading the reptiles from their winter home into a summer observatory where they could be viewed. The zookeeper is quoted as saying that alligators and crocodiles had an "epicurean fondness for the black man."[88]

- A 1923 *Time* magazine article claims that children in Chipley, Florida were being used as gator bait. According to the article, expert marksman would wait, while a tied up, crying Black child lured alligators. Once the gators approached the children, the marksman would fire, killing the alligator.

- A *Miami New Times* article describes the same scene but adds that the marksmen would wait until the alligators had clamped their jaws around the baby.[89]

- In October 1919, the *Richmond Times Dispatch* printed what may be a joke titled, "Game Protection." It reads, "We understand the Florida authorities are going to prohibit the use of live pickaninnies as alligator bait. They say they've got to do something to check the rapid disappearance of the alligator through indigestion."

---

88   Foxworth (2016)
89   Strouse (2014)

- A January 1922 advertisement for the Brown County Fair in the Minnesota newspaper the *New Ulm Review* reads, "there will also be a big colored alligator pursuing a fleeing pickaninny, and many other beautiful designs."

The amount of memorabilia, including pictures and postcards showing Black babies being chased and eaten by alligators suggests that it's something some white people once considered to be funny, and it led to other horrific behavior.

A man named Johnny Lee Gaddy recently shared with researcher, Dr. Antoinette Harrell, that in 1957 he witnessed Black children being fed to the hogs on the campus of the infamous Arthur G. Dozier Reform School in the Florida Panhandle.[90] According to Gaddy, he came across a severed human hand when feeding the hogs, and surmised that the school was cooking Black children to feed the hogs. The Dozier school became infamous when a mass grave was discovered on its grounds, filled with the bodies of children who had died on its campus and were interred without identification.

Blacks and Medical Malpractice

There is a long history of medical malpractice dating back at least to the 1600s, where Black people were used for scientific experiments without their informed consent. The experiments on syphilitic patients at Tuskegee gained some infamy when it was revealed that doctors were using unknowing Black men to study the progression of syphilis in 1972,[91] but there are many more examples of how science has failed Black people. Here are some of the most infamous cases:

---

90   Henry (2019)
91   Gordon (2014)

- Doctors from the US Public Health service wanting to track
  the natural progression of syphilis studied a group of mostly
  poor illiterate Black men who had been infected with the
  disease. Even worse, they withheld the cure from the men after
  penicillin became an effective treatment for the disease in the
  1930s. The study went on for four decades.

- In 2014, Centers for Disease Control and Prevention
  doctors withheld information from Black parents about an
  MMR vaccine that was shown to increase the likelihood of
  Black children developing regressive autism by three times.
  Particularly at risk were Black children who participated in the
  study of the new vaccine and were injected with it before the
  age of three.

- During slavery there were numerous experiments performed
  on enslaved people, but the most notorious may be an
  experiment performed by Dr. J. Marion Sims who is known
  as the father of modern gynecology. He performed surgery
  on patients with vesico-vaginal fistulas, an extremely painful
  condition, without any anesthesia, because, he said during a
  lecture in 1857, "The operations weren't painful enough to
  justify the trouble" of anesthetizing his patients.

- Henrietta Lacks was unsuccessfully treated for cervical cancer
  during the 1950s. When doctors removed her cervix, they used
  cells from it to clone the first "immortal" cells. Doctors have
  cloned nearly twenty tons of Lacks's cells since removing them.
  This was unethical, because not only did researchers clone the
  cells without her knowledge, they also published her family's
  medical records without their consent.[92]

- Twenty-year-old Sarah Baartman was put on display as part
  of a freak show exhibit that toured Europe as the "Venus
  Hottentots." The word "Hottentot" was once used to describe
  Khoi people, but is considered to be racist today. She

---

92 Rothman (2017)

unsuccessfully sued for her freedom and was held for scientific and medical experimentation. After her death, her brains and sexual organs were removed and put on public display as part of an exhibit at the Musée L'Homme in Paris.

- Fannie Lou Hamer, a pioneer in the Civil Rights Movement, was sterilized unbeknownst to her by her white doctor.[93]

- Just recently, research showed that Black babies under white doctor care are more likely to die.[94]

The unethical use of Black people for research purposes has led to some significant problems for Black people and the medical community. Because of mistrust of the system, Black people are less likely to volunteer as study participants. This has also led to slower advances in medicine to address conditions Black people are more susceptible to.

Racist Songs

The ubiquitous ice cream truck song "Turkey in the Straw" is an example of children's songs with a racist past. While "Turkey in the Straw," in its original version is harmless, the song was co-opted during the minstrel years and its lyrics changed to "Nigger Loves a Watermelon Ha! Ha! Ha!" So every time you hear the ice cream truck in your neighborhood playing that song, you can think back to its not-so-innocent past as a tune meant to poke fun at Black people.

It's hardly the only children's song with a racist past.[95] Here are some others:

---

93   "Fannie Lou Hamer" (2020)

94   "The Impact of Racism on Children's Health" (2020)

95   Abad-Santos (2014)

- "Eenie-Meenie-Minie-Mo" originally had the lyrics, "catch a nigger by his toe" as part of the song. It was meant to make fun of runaway slaves and what to do with them if they're caught and holler (Let him go or make him pay twenty dollars every day).

- "Oh! Susannah" is a caricaturization of a Black person who is so stupid they can't grasp meteorology or geography (sun so hot I froze to death).

- "Jimmy Crack Corn" is sung in the voice of a slave whose master has died. Some say that the slave is rejoicing at his master's death, but other critics argue it still has a racist past.

- The lyrics to the song "Pick a Bale of Cotton" go: "Jump down, turn around, pick a bale of cotton. Gotta jump down, turn around, oh, Lordie, pick a bale a day." This can be seen as glorifying and making fun of slave conditions.

- Lyricist Stephen Foster deliberately used his lyrics in "Camptown Races" to mimic Black speech, and in doing so, managed to poke fun at Blacks. The lyrics to the song go: "De Camptown ladies sing dis song—Doo-dah! Doo-dah!/ I come down dah wid my hat caved in—Doo-dah! Doo-dah!/ I go back home wid a pocket full of tin—Oh! Doo-dah day!"

Some of these songs are still performed by children's choirs at school pageants. For the most part, educators change the lyrics of the songs so that they aren't offensive. Experts disagree on whether it is right or not to change the songs so that they're harmless, because it may be erasing history to do so. But you can always teach your children the updated versions of the song and then, when they are ready and can understand history, explain the origins of the songs and their racist pasts.

Racist Commercials

In 2020, Uncle Ben's Rice and Aunt Jemimah Pancake Syrup
made the headlines with news that these products were changing
their labels because of a racist history attached to the imagery they
used. These products are just two of many products that have used
stereotypical imagery of Black people. If you do an image search for
racist commercials, your feed will be filled with plenty of images
from the late nineteenth and early twentieth century for bleach
and other products that show Black people caricatured on product
labels; often Black children are fool-hearty, grinning jesters pleased
with the products. Keep an eye on the shelves at your local grocery
store. Some of the products out there may not have been recalled for
racist imagery, and it will give you an opportunity to show your kids
how Black people have been portrayed in the past, and why it's not
acceptable marketing in today's world.

Racist Objects

There is a large quantity of racist memorabilia still floating around
in the world. They come in all shapes and sizes from ashtrays to
matchbooks to cookie jars, all depicting Blacks as "coons, sambos,
Uncle Toms, mammies, and pickaninnies." Many are in the hands
of private collectors, but there is a Jim Crow Museum of Racist
Memorabilia at Ferris State University that collects these objects in
the hopes that tolerance can be taught through an examination of
our intolerant past.[96] The history of the objects paints a clear picture
of how Blacks have been caricatured and stereotyped in the years
following slavery. Prices for these items have skyrocketed on eBay
over the past twenty years or so, mainly because they are becoming
rarer and harder to find.

---

96 Pilgrim (n.d.)

Should we pretend the past didn't happen?

All over the world, calls to remove monuments that glorify a racist and imperialist past are happening.[97] Whether it's a statue of Robert E. Lee or one of Christopher Columbus, people are gathering in opposition to monuments. Some people argue that destroying these monuments is erasing history and that they should remain up to preserve a past nearly no one thinks we should relive, but the central questions about these monuments should be: Are they preserving history? Or are they glorifying a horrific chapter in our collective past?[98]

As monuments fall, how do we reckon with a racist past?[99] One way to do so is to erect new monuments to people who championed for good in the face of racism and fought for justice in the face of injustice. A monument is not preserving history if it is making a hero out of a tyrant, and we aren't likely to learn much by glorifying tyrants. One way to approach the issue right now is to teach your children the truth about the people behind these monuments and teach them that some people still look up to them as heroes. But the best way to teach your kids about history is to find role models they can look up to, who represent ideals you'd like them to learn and practice.

All of the remnants of our racist past are just a piece of the history of systemic racism.[100] Whether or not they are preserved, the history will not go away, but it's up to you to educate your children about the things they probably won't be taught in their schools.

---

97   McLaughlin (2020)

98   Bishara (2020)

99   Morris (2020)

100   Jacob (2010)

Chapter 8

Microaggressions, "Reverse Racism," and Intersectionality

Now let's discuss microaggressions (what they are, and how to disarm them), commonly used phrases that are actually racist, what to do if non-Black friends say racist things, and how to respond to micro-aggressive acts. We'll also discuss intersectionality, what it is, and why it's important to understand.

Microaggressions

Microaggressions are some of the most stressful parts of being a person of color, because they never seem to stop, they come at you from everywhere, and they are difficult to respond to. The different ways that a microaggression can sneak into your day are stunning, and they are sometimes hard to recognize. Some of them are so subtle you find yourself asking if it was a microaggression at all or if you imagined it. In this chapter, we'll look at different types of microaggressions and suggest ways you and your children can respond to them. Let's start by defining them.

Definitions

Microaggressions are the daily interactions people of color and other marginalized groups of people face that reinforce a bias or a stereotype.[101] These interactions may be intentional or unconscious. They may be verbal interactions or nonverbal encounters. Micro-assaults, micro-insults, and micro-invalidation are all types of microaggression. In the next few pages, I will give specific examples, and provide ways to address each of these specific situations.

Micro-assaults are explicit uses of a derogatory term used to harm or hurt an intended victim through either name-calling, avoidant behavior, or intentional discriminatory practices. (Some people will cite using racial epithets, displaying the Confederate flag, or serving a white patron before a Black patron as examples of micro-assaults, but those are pretty blatant and overt incidents of racism, if you ask me.)

In this excerpt of his viral Facebook post, Brian Crooks tells the story of going to a friend's house in eighth grade to jump on his trampoline:

> I didn't know the kid all that well, but we had some mutual friends and at that age, if a kid has a trampoline, you're going to jump on that trampoline. He had a couple of neighbors who were probably six or seven-year-old girls. We're jumping on the trampoline and the girls come out of their house and come over into his yard. Within about five minutes, they were laughing while saying, 'Get off our property, Black *boy*.' They were little, and they were laughing, so I don't think they knew how ugly they were being. After all, they'd probably never had a Black kid in their one or two elementary school classes. But they'd clearly heard that phrase somewhere else before. I wasn't even on their property; I was next door. But it's fair to assume that at some point, someone in their house had said, "Get off my property, Black *boy*."

---

101   DeAngelis (2009)

Micro-assaults are most likely deliberate, but usually occur in private circumstances to avoid repercussions for bad behavior and to maintain a degree of anonymity. Some people call this "old-fashioned racism."

Micro-insults are a type of communication that is rude and insensitive and demeans a person's racial or cultural heritage. These are very subtle snubs that even the perpetrator may not recognize as harmful, but they convey a clear insult to the person of color. An example of this would be when a non-Black person asks a Black employee, "How did you manage to get this job?" because it implies the Black employee is not qualified for the position.

This segment from Brian Crooks's viral Facebook post illustrates micro-insulting behavior from his driving instructor:

> "When I was going through driver's ed, my behind-the-wheel instructor was a football coach at one of the other Naperville high schools. He asked what kind of car I wanted one time, and I told him I was gonna get my dad's Dodge Intrepid, but that I really liked my brother's Mazda. He looked at me like I was nuts and said he figured I'd want an Impala, so I could put some hydraulics on it and 'hit dem switchezzzzz.' When we got back to my house at the end of my last behind-the-wheel session, he shook my hand and said it was a pleasure teaching me how to drive. Then, he said, 'You're a Black kid, but you're pretty cool, you know? Like, you're not like one of *those* Black people, you know?' "

Microinvalidations are a kind of communication that excludes, negates, or renders null the thoughts, feelings, and experiences of a person of color. For example, complimenting an Asian woman on their use of the English language and then asking where she was born is a micro-invalidation if the woman was born in the US, because it negates her American heritage.

In his poignant account on Facebook, Brian gives an example of micro-invalidation as well:

Brian played football in high school, and one of the other kids on the team had been friends with him since middle school. They weren't best friends, but ran in the same circles and were friendly with each other. When Brian was sixteen or seventeen, the friend started referring to him as "The Whitest Black guy." It really pissed Brian off and the other kid knew it irked him. Because Brian used proper grammar, wore clothes that fit, and listened to heavy metal in addition to hip hop, it made him "white" in the other kid's mindset. To the other kid, being authentically Black meant behaving like a caricature of how a Black person should behave.

This two-minute video on microaggressions (www.youtube.com/watch?v=hDd3bzA7450) discusses the impact they have on people of color. It's a great video to watch with your teenager because it allows you to ask them how overhearing a racial slur might have an impact on them.

The Art of the Comeback

Microaggressions are made up of two parts:

1. The surface-level communication or words spoken (what the person actually says).

2. The unconscious meta-communication or the message that the microaggression delivers. (You can think of this as how the microaggression is received by a Black person.)

Teach your children that it can be difficult to know how to respond to a microaggression, and to decide whether they should respond at all.[102]

And while your child should try as best they can to be patient with perpetrators of microaggressions—if they remain calm, they'll feel more in control than anything else—they should also acknowledge the validity of their feelings. Microaggressions will make them angry, and they should not ignore this anger.

While some of the tools given in this chapter can be used for de-escalation in certain situations, let's be clear: we Black people don't have to constantly diffuse the fire. We must learn to validate Black anger, including our own, and express this anger. Sometimes being peaceful citizens works against speaking up for ourselves and for our children. Sometimes being polite simply doesn't work.

Teach your children strategies for dealing with common microaggressions.

Words: "Don't blame me. I never owned slaves."

Why it's offensive: The statement negates Black suffering even after slaves were emancipated, and it implicitly denies white responsibility for the systemic racial issues in society today.[103]

How to respond:

> Regardless of whether you personally owned slaves, much of the wealth and infrastructure of this country was built by Black labor, and white people continue to benefit from a system of racism that grants them many privileges. We all inherited a racist system from the forefathers of this nation. It is everyone's responsibility to create equal justice. When you say that you never owned slaves, it shows

---

102   "10 Things NEVER to Say to a Black Coworker" (2009); "Examples of Racial Microaggressions" (n.d.); Hales (2020); Norman (2013); Rogers (2020); Ward (2020)

103   "But I Never Owned Any Slaves" (2014); Staunton (2008)

that you don't understand how hard it is for people like me to grow up with systemic racism, and you're belittling my experiences as a Black person.

Words: "White privilege doesn't exist."

Why it's offensive: It nullifies Black experience and leaves an implication that if there is no white privilege, systemic racism is not a problem in society.

How to respond:

You can grab a donut at 7-Eleven and while you walk around with it in your hand, looking at beverages, people still assume you are paying for your snack. That's a privilege that makes your life that much safer, one that a Black person like me doesn't have. In a racist system, people assume Black people are criminals and that white people will pay. The presumption that you will stay in integrity as a white person is because of the color of your skin, not because of anything you did for your reputation. You did nothing as a white person to be presumed innocent except be born in a system that is racist.

And for the people saying "not all whites are racist," know that you are *part* of a "racist" system. You participate in this system that perpetuates racism whether you are aware of it or not. And if you're white and this doesn't make sense, you need to do more work. Please do the work and get curious.

Words: "All lives matter."

Why it's offensive: It nullifies the experiences of Black people whose lives did not matter, like George Floyd, or Philando Castile.[104]

---

104   Baker (2020); Capatides (2020); Kelly (2020); Shahvisi (2020); Smith (2020); "Saying 'All Lives Matter' " (2020)

How to respond:

Brian Crooks explains perfectly why we say, "Black Lives Matter":

> When we say, 'Black Lives Matter,' understand what that actually
> means. We aren't saying that *only* Black Lives Matter. We're saying,
> 'Black Lives Matter *too*.' For the entirety of the history of this country,
> Black lives have not mattered. At a minimum, they haven't mattered
> nearly as much as white lives. If a Black person kills another Black
> person, and we have it on tape, the killer goes to jail. If a white police
> officer kills a Black person and we have it on tape, the entire judicial
> system steps up to make sure that officer doesn't go to jail. It doesn't
> matter whether the Black person was holding a toy gun in a Walmart,
> or whether the Black person was a twelve-year-old kid playing with a
> BB gun in an empty park. The police union steps up to say the officer
> was fearing for his life, just worried about trying to make it home
> that night. IF a grand jury is convened, the prosecutor will present
> a purposely weak case to make sure no indictment is reached. IF,
> by some miracle, an indictment is handed down, no jury is actually
> going to convict that officer. That's what we mean when we say Black
> Lives Matter.

Words: "I'm not racist. I have a Black friend." | "I'm not a racist. I
have several Black friends."

Why it's offensive: People have historically used the phrase to cover
up racist behavior. Having a Black friend doesn't give you a "get out
of racism free" card.[105] It treats Black people as though they are some
kind of token object. We still see people try to defend insensitive or
racist remarks by posting photos of themselves with Black people as if
that immediately excuses their behavior.

How to respond:

> When you say, "I have Black friends" as an excuse to absolve you of
> your behavior, you are belittling the word "friendship." Black people

---

105   Dennis (2016)

are not monoliths, and there is no official Black seal of approval. Rather than leaning on your Black friendships to excuse your behavior, it would be more constructive if you thought of the ways your words and actions impact your Black friends and Black people you don't know all that well, and work to fight racism rather than engage in it.

Words: "Can I touch your hair?" | "Is that your real hair?"

Why it's offensive: There are several reasons asking to touch a Black person's hair is offensive, but the main reason is that it doesn't respect boundaries.[106] In the same way you wouldn't ask a stranger if you could touch her breasts, it's just unacceptable to ask to touch a stranger's hair or ask questions about it. It also exoticizes Black hair and places the Black person in a position of being "othered." Black people report that people often touch their hair even without asking permission.[107]

How to respond:

> When you ask if you can touch my hair, you seem to think I'm in a circus sideshow. I don't wear my hair this way for your amusement, and it is absolutely not okay to touch me in any way.

In this excerpt of his story, Brian Crooks tells of his own experiencing with having his hair touched:

> From elementary school through middle school, I can't remember how many times the white kids asked if they could touch my hair. I'm not kidding when I say it happened pretty much once a week at least. At first, it didn't bother me. But eventually, I felt like an exhibit in a petting zoo. And I didn't have the vocabulary to explain to them that it was really weird that they kept asking to touch my hair all the time. See, I was a pretty shy kid. I was the only Black one, I was overweight, and I'd moved three times before I turned ten. So, rather than tell the white

---

106 Akyianu (2019); Mukando (2020); Opiah (2013); Osterheldt (2016)
107 "Don't Touch My Hair" (2020); Yeboah (2019)

kids that no, they couldn't rummage through my hair, I just said yes and sat there quietly while they marveled at how my hair felt.

Words: "I'm color-blind." | "When I look at you, I don't see color." | "America is a melting pot." | "There is only one race, the human race."

Why it's offensive: Unless the perpetrator is blind or literally color-blind, they absolutely see color. What a person is saying when they say, "I don't see color" is that they are viewing the world through a position of privilege and can ignore injustices that are based on skin color.[108]

How to respond:

When you say, "I don't see color when I look at you," it shows you don't see me at all. I'm Black, and no amount of color-blindness is going to change that fact, and what it means for me as a Black person. You can say something like that only because you are in a position of privilege where your own skin color doesn't affect you in the same ways mine does. Rather than not seeing my color, I wish you would look more closely at what it means to be Black and how it affects me and people like me.

Words: "You are so articulate." | "You are pretty for a Black girl." | "You're not really Black." | "I don't think of you as Black." | "Why are you acting white?" | "You don't sound like other Black people."

Why it's offensive: Where do we start with this one? The problem with these microaggressions is that they single out an individual as superior to the rest of their race.[109] "You're articulate" implies that most Black people cannot speak clearly and intelligently.[110] "You're

---

108 Asare (2019); Chaffers (2019); Ferlazzo (2020); Helligar (2020); Hill (2020); Louie (2016); Pavlovitz (2016); Scruggs (2009); Shelton (2020); Whitfield (2020); Wingfield (2015)

109 Bond 2014

110 Desmond-Harris (2017); Marshall (2020); McCowan, (2016); McKenzie (2019); McWorther (2014, 2019); Tough (2004)

pretty for a Black girl" is straight up saying that most Black women are not attractive.[111] These are all back-handed compliments. There is no one way a Black person looks or speaks or acts, so to point out the differences means that the perpetrator is saying, "you are different" while simultaneously insulting the rest of your race.

How to respond:

> When I hear you say [insert offensive phrase here], I'm not hearing that as a compliment. I'm hearing that you think other Black people are inarticulate (or ugly, or different, or stupid), and that's deeply insulting to me. Black people are all very different and to lump us all together into one group based on some people's traits is very demeaning and stereotypical. It tells me that you don't see people as individuals. You should get to know us better.

Words: "As a woman, I know what you go through as a racial minority."

Why it's offensive: While sexism is a serious issue, the problem of racism affects both people of all genders and the experiences are vastly different. In addition, Black women may have to deal with both the experiences of sexism and racism. Even if a white woman is sometimes discriminated against for her gender, she still has the privilege of being white.

How to respond:

> Sexism is a terrible problem, and I understand that it can be difficult, but the issue of racism is more complex than what you think, and even if you have had some bad experiences with sexism, you still have the privilege that comes with being white, so they are not the same thing. For example, if you are pulled over by the police, you can just hand over your license and registration and the matter is cleared up in a few minutes. For me, there is a lot more that goes into a police

---

111   Abbensetts (n.d).; Carroll (2016); Crews (2016); Fletcher (2020); Stephens (2020); Tutu (2017)

encounter. Black people are discriminated against in this society on every level, and that's not something you can understand simply because you are a woman.

Words: "I believe the most qualified person should get the job." | "Everyone can succeed in this society, if they work hard enough."

Why it's offensive: Black people are far less likely to receive job offers even when they are as qualified as white applicants. Studies have shown that people with Black sounding names receive fewer callbacks, and that a white person with a criminal history is more likely to receive a call for a job than a Black person with no criminal history.

How to respond:

> Ideally the best qualified person would get the job, but if you do some research, you'll discover that there is a vast disparity in how many Black applicants get calls for jobs, even when their resumes show they are better qualified to do the work. When you say that, it belies the facts of the matter.

Words: (asking a Black person) "Why do you have to be so loud / animated? Just calm down." | "Why are you so angry?"

Why it's offensive: Historically, Black people have been told to be quiet, and seen as violent if they express any anger at all. The subtle message being given is "sit down and shut up."

How to respond:

> When you say that, it tells me you don't understand how upsetting it is to be told to be quiet and settle down. I have a right to express my feelings on this issue. How would you like it if someone told you that you couldn't express your anger?

Words: Imitating accents or dialects.

Why it's offensive: Historically, Black people have been mocked for their accents and manner of speech in popular media and in minstrel shows. It's stereotyping and often done to make fun of a perceived lack of intelligence and to portray Blacks as thugs, idiots or clowns.

How to respond:

> When you make fun of Black people by imitating their accents, you are perpetuating a harmful stereotype that doesn't show the diversity and intelligence of Black people. I find it offensive.

Words: "I'm not racist, but…"

Why it's offensive: A good deal of why this statement is offensive is contingent on what follows the "but." However, it is safe to assume that something racist is about to spill out of the perpetrator's mouth.[112] The "but" is an attempt to make an exception to racist beliefs and to convince you that a little bit of racism is all right.

How to respond:

> I know you think you're not racist, but what you just said was very racist. We live in a racist society; it's impossible for you as a white person not to be even a little racist. Rather than qualifying your beliefs, why don't you do something to fight racism? You could call your local politicians, or join me at a protest, or support an organization that fights racism. Simply telling me you're not racist isn't good enough. Show me you're anti-racist."

Words: "Oh, you should meet my friend Devon. He's Black too."

Why it's offensive: This is similar to the "I have a Black friend" microaggression.[113] It's offensive because it tokenizes a Black person, often to cover racist behavior.

---

112   Paul (2020); Vaughan (2020)
113   Blay (2017)

How to respond:

> I'm sure Devon is a lovely person, but I'm wondering if you think I should meet him because we have something in common or because he's Black?

Words: Calling a Black woman or man "sister" or "brother," respectively. Or worse: "My nigga"

Why it's offensive: This microaggression is used to create a false feeling of allyship. It's offensive because it relies on stereotypical and sometimes offensive language.

How to respond:

> I'd prefer you not call me that. I find it offensive because it reinforces stereotypes. My name is_____. You can call me that.

These following last three examples are in the gray area that exists between microaggression and overt racism. Examples of this kind are prevalent in the day-to-day lives of Black people. In fact, in September of 2020, University of Michigan at Dearborn was heavily criticized for sponsoring a non-POC (people of color) Zoom event for white students to discuss racism[114]. The issue with the event is that it didn't give Black students the opportunity to weigh in on issues that impact them directly.

Words: "Do you eat a lot of…"

Why it's offensive: It makes an assumption that all Black people eat the same thing and that there isn't a vast variety of cultures among Black people, and varied cuisines.

---

114 Linly (2020)

How to respond:

> When you ask me that question it makes me wonder if you are being racist or just plain ignorant. Black people eat all different kinds of foods, the same way white people do.

In this portion of his Facebook post, Brian Crooks writes about the pressure he felt being singled out:

> My least favorite time of the year, every year, was February. Black History Month. Being the only Black kid in the class, I was the designated reader for the entire month. When it came time to read from our history books about slavery and the Triangle Trade Route, I was always the one who was chosen to read. When it came time to read about Jim Crow, it was my turn. George Washington Carver and the peanut? That sounds like a job for Brian. Booker T. Washington? Harriet Tubman? Surely Brian is the perfect choice for those passages. All the while, I felt the eyes of my fellow students on me. Again, I was already a shy kid. So, having an entire classroom of white kids stare at me while I explained what lynching and Black Codes were was pretty mortifying.

Words: "You people…"

Why it's offensive: It's a statement that marginalizes Black people and places them in an "other" category that is separate and unequal to the majority.

How to respond:

> When you say, "you people," I feel I am being disrespected for my color and cultural group and that is hurtful. Black people aren't just one monolithic group, we are vastly different individuals. If you took the time to meet and get to know us, you might be able to see us as individuals."

In this excerpt of his Facebook post, Brian Crooks talks more about the kind of racist incidents that shaped his life:

> "Back at Iowa, things were pretty cool. Yeah, the occasional frat boy would call me a nigger when he was mad at me at the bar, but I had a lot of good friends and it's not like nobody had ever called me that before or anything. I was dating a girl when I went to college, and we broke up right before my sophomore year. She made sure to tell me she would *never* date someone outside of her race again when we broke up. As though A) I was the representative of all Black people, and B) I was going to have to explain to all Black men why she was unwilling to date them in the future."

Words: "But, but, but, what about black-on-black gun violence, huh?! What do you have to say about that?!"

Why it's offensive: Black people kill other Black people at about the same per capita rate as white people kill people of their own race. This argument is most often used to minimize the issue of police brutality. It's a non sequitur; violence among Blacks has nothing to do with police brutality or racial violence.

How to respond:

> Black communities have programs to fight the violence in their neighborhoods. This is a separate issue. I'd suggest you educate yourself about the rates of Black-on-Black violence if it's a topic that interests you, but I'm hearing you use it as an excuse for other violence, and that is unacceptable.

Speak up when you hear racist language or stereotyping, or witness racist behavior. If it is not a safe situation, wait until it is safe, and then speak to your child about the experience. Look at racist encounters as an opportunity to teach your child about self-advocacy.

Everyday Expressions that are Actually Racist

There are a number of everyday, commonly used expressions that are actually offensive and racist that you might not even be aware are racist. It's important to root these expressions out of your own usage—and that of your children—and to be aware of when others are overusing them so that you can point out the racism to them.[115]

White trash: This expression is used to describe poor white people, often who live in trailer parks and are loud and crude. The problem is that using the term "white" in conjunction with "trash" implies that whites are not normally trashy, whereas it would be common for people of color to be considered "trash."

Black sheep: It's used to refer to an outcast, but tying the color "black" to a negative term, or any implication of darkness and light as a means of judging good or bad is problematic and racist.

Sold down the river: This expression is used to mean that someone has been double-crossed. It comes from the days of slavery when a slave who misbehaved would be sold to a plantation with a cruel owner to be beaten and whipped.

Peanut gallery: This expression is used to refer to armchair critics who always seem to have a negative opinion about everything. But it comes from a term used during vaudeville to describe the seating area where Blacks would sit because the seats were less expensive. Back in those days, if the audience didn't like the performance, rather than throw rotten fruit they'd toss peanuts.

Urban: It's still acceptable to refer to a congested city center as urban, but the term has been linked to Black music, which isn't accurate and

---

115 Helligar (2020)

has come to be considered offensive. Even the Grammys have banned the word "urban" from its recording categories.

Antebellum: Technically this word means "before the war," and is not offensive if it is just referring to the period before the Civil War. The problem is that it has been used to glorify the Southern mansions and plantation lifestyle (think hoop-skirted women like Scarlett O'Hara).

Thug: The word used to just mean "hoodlum," but nowadays it's picked up a more racist connotation and is used almost exclusively to refer to Black adolescents and young men.

Uppity: This expression used to be followed most often by the "n" word and is used to describe Blacks who don't know how to "stay in their place" or who speak up too loudly about issues that upset them. Rush Limbaugh referred to both Barack and Michelle Obama as uppity. A better word to use if you need to use it at all is "snob."

Teach your kid to watch their word choice. Also teach them not to make any blanketed assumptions about other groups of people. Let your kids learn to see people as individuals and encourage them to strive for individuality. Teach them that people are dynamic and interesting in their diversity.

What to do if your child's non-Black friends keep saying the wrong things about racism?

It can be difficult for non-Black people to talk about racism. The subject has been taboo for many of them for most of their lives, and they are just learning the vocabulary to clearly and openly speak up about racism. And we *want* non-Black people to speak out about racism. But what do you do if your child's friends just don't get it right? What if they insist that "all lives matter"?[116]

Tell your child to get better friends.

Ha! Just kidding. But remember, first, it's not your child's responsibility to educate non-Black people on racism. If non-Black people are sincere in wanting to find out more, they can do the research themselves, and constantly fielding questions or trying to raise awareness can wear your child out and may have some psychological repercussions.

The best thing you and your child can do is be honest about how racism impacts you and raise awareness of why what these friends are saying is hurtful. For example, "All Lives Matter." You can tell them that all lives *should* matter, but that Black people are killed in racist actions more often than any other race, and so until Black Lives Matter equally, "All Lives Matter" is not a true statement. You can tell them how it makes you feel when they continue to say, "all lives matter." But come at it from the standpoint of raising awareness, not educating them or telling them how to behave.

Make it clear to your child: "If you feel someone is really trying to learn, you may want to cut them some slack, but if they are hard-lined about the issue, it may be best to let them go, and focus your energy elsewhere."

In this portion of his public Facebook post, Brian Crooks relates the frustration of living under systemic racism:

> White people often say that we make everything about race. That's because, for us, damn near everything *is* about race. It's always been that way. When I have a great phone interview, but go for my in-person interview only to be told that the position has been filled,

---

how am I supposed to know that's not just because they expected a White Iowa graduate to show up for the interview? When I have an especially attentive employee keep checking in with me at the mall, how am I supposed to know they're shooting for employee of the month, not watching me to make sure I'm not stealing? What do you think it's like when someone says 'You don't sound Black at all' when I have a phone conversation with them and then meet them in person? What do you think it's like seeing Confederate flags on cars and flag poles in Northern states, only to have someone tell me I'm being too sensitive for not liking it?

Actions...and How to Respond

The type of microaggression known as a micro-assault can be the most difficult to deal with. Sometimes you'll find yourself questioning whether a microaggression just occurred because they can be very subtle. But sometimes they are so blatant you just can't believe one occurred and are at a loss as to what to do.

Here are some suggestions for dealing with micro-assaults and more flagrant acts of racism. This list will be helpful to both you and your child.

Action: Calling you the wrong (other Black person's) name: "Oh, sorry, wrong person!"

Message: "You all look alike" or "I can't be bothered to learn your name."

How to respond: Correct them. Say, "My name is _____." If it's an ongoing problem, pull the person to the side and tell them, "I don't think you understand how much it bothers me that you haven't learned my name. I'd appreciate it if you'd stop calling me _____. My name is _____."

Action: Clutching their purse, dodging while passing a black man or unnecessarily calling the police.

Message: Black people want to rob, rape, assault, or otherwise harm me.

How to respond: Depending on the situation, you might need to just back away; put your hands where they are visible and leave the scene. If the person is calling the police, you can say, "I have no intention of harming you. I'm leaving now." If the encounter escalates at all, pull out your cell phone and record the incident.

Action: A store owner following a customer of color around the store.

Message: Black people steal things from my store. They are suspicious.

How to respond: Your instinct might be to do your business elsewhere, but remember that in an equal world, you should be able to do business *anywhere.*

You have options:

You can calmly confront the owner and use technology to document the interaction. If you don't capture the moment, or you wait until you get home to report the incident, chances are you won't be believed by Management or Headquarters; it's he said/she said at that point. It's a sad truth but, in this world, you need to learn how to document using video evidence.

Another option is to ignore the situation and continue your shopping (while avoiding putting your hands in your pocket or purse). Then, check out of the store and leave. If you find it best not to confront a suspicious store owner or security guard as it could cause the situation to escalate, that's your choice—and yours alone—to make. (Many parents will encourage their children to go that route.)

Action: Dismissing an individual who brings up race / culture in work / school setting.

Message: This is not an issue we feel comfortable discussing or, worse, there is no problem here.

How to respond: If you are the person being dismissed, take a deep breath, remain calm, and say:

> When you dismiss my concerns, it makes me feel like I'm not being heard. I know these issues can be difficult to talk about, but this is important to me.

And then continue.

If it is someone else being dismissed, you can speak up and say:

> I'm interested in hearing what _____ has to say. Let's hear them out.

Action: Person of color mistaken for a service worker.

Message: People of color don't get better jobs than service positions.

How to respond: "I don't work here."

Action: Having a taxicab pass a person of color and pick up a white passenger, or being ignored at a store counter as attention is given to the white customer behind you.

Message: The white customer has preferential treatment and should be waited on first.

How to respond: Speak up decisively. "Excuse me, I was waiting here." If the clerk doesn't respond, ask to speak to a manager. You can also contact the Better Business Bureau.

Action: A college or university with buildings that are all names after white heterosexual upper-class males.

Message: White upper-class heterosexual males are the only people who have contributed to the college's growth.

How to respond: Organize a protest and a petition drive to have some of the building names changed to reflect the diversity of the university. Contact the president of the university and let them know you feel the names should reflect a wider diversity of alumni.

Action: Television shows and movies that feature predominantly white people, without representation of people of color.

Message: Only white people are entertaining.

How to respond: Change the channel. Find programs with a diverse cast. Write the television station and let them know you would like more programs with people of color.

Action: Overcrowding of public schools in communities of color.

Message: Black children don't deserve the same kinds of facilities that non-Black children enjoy.

How to respond: Get involved with school board meetings. Petition the board to do a study for overcrowding. Contact your local politicians and write them letters about the overcrowding. Form a coalition of parents to address the issue with the school.

Microaggressions are painful.

Here, Brian Crooks explains the toll microaggressions (and overt racism) can take on a person of color:

> I could go on and on and on about this. I could tell you about the guy who wanted to buy his guitar from someone who 'actually knew what a guitar was' when I worked at Guitar Center. At that point, I had a

Gibson Les Paul at my house and an Ibanez acoustic, plus a Warwick fretless bass. I could tell you about the coworker who thought it was funny to adopt a stereotypical Black accent to apologize that we weren't going to have fried chicken and cornbread at our company Christmas party. I could tell you about the time I gave my floor mate a haircut freshman year and he 'thanked' me by saying he'd let a negro cut his hair any day of the week. I could tell you about leaving a bar heartbroken and fighting tears when the Trayvon Martin verdict came out only to see a couple middle-aged white guys high-fiving and saying he 'got what he deserved' right outside. These are only a handful of the experiences I've had in my thirty-one years.

The Myth of Reverse Racism

We often hear from white people who claim that they have been discriminated against. They say things like: "You know what? I've been discriminated against too. I experienced 'reverse racism' so don't talk to me about racism." Or "The way you talk about white people makes you a racist!" or "Why don't we have a White History Month?"

The problem with this argument is that it shows a lack of understanding about what racism is and how it operates. It comes down to the difference between systematic oppression and hurt feelings. White people can be discriminated against, yes. There are some bigots who hate all white people, yes, but it's not racism. The difference is that white people are in a position of privilege when it comes to race. We don't need a White History Month, because every month is White History Month. One only needs to open up a history textbook to see which is the dominant culture. The equation is this:

Racism = oppression + power.

Black people have never been in a position of power where they can oppress white people, so reverse racism is just a myth, just hurt feelings.[117]

The argument of reverse racism most frequently comes up when Affirmative Action programs are discussed, and at the root of the problem is a grievous misunderstanding about how these programs work.[118] One need only look at the statistics to see that Black people aren't taking away college degrees or jobs from white people. Blacks, on the contrary, are less likely to earn a college degree and more likely to be unemployed after college. The myth is just based on an unfounded fear of losing privilege. And if you are accustomed to having privilege, losing it can feel like discrimination and racism. But it's not.

Alexia LaFata wrote in the *Elite Daily*, "There has never, ever, ever been a national set of laws or system put in place to systematically oppress white people or push them to a status that is 'less than.' Not once. Ever. So 'reverse racism' can truly never exist."[119]

Intersectionality

Kimberlé Crenshaw first laid out her theory of intersectionality in a 1989 paper she wrote titled, "Demarginalizing the Intersection of Race and Sex." In her paper, she argued that oppression and discrimination is a multi-faceted problem not limited to just Black vs. white, but complicated by other features such as gender. So for example, a Black woman not only faces issues of racism determined by her skin color, she is also further challenged by sexism due to her gender.

---

117   Lewis (2016); Manisha (2016); "Reverse Racism" (n.d.)
118   Newkirk II (2017)
119   Lewis (2016)

There are a number of factors that intersect for every individual, some of these attributes are an advantage, some a disadvantage, and we all experience intersectionality and personal power to varying degrees based on these factors. Some of these key factors include age, gender, economic status, ethnicity and culture, physical (dis)ability, education level, personal politics, religion and sexual orientation. Understanding intersectionality helps people understand one another more clearly, and helps people find common ground.[120]

Let's look at a white man, who is gay, and has a physical disability. He is privileged in the sense that he is white, but his sexual orientation and disability are two areas where he is prone to oppression. Now let's look at a Black woman who is young, able-bodied and highly educated. Being Black and female are two areas where she is prone to oppression, but being young, highly educated and able-bodied are all areas where she has some privilege.

Intersectionality is not a means to measure other people and make judgments based on how certain factors intersect, but it can be a useful tool in understanding how oppression works at differing levels based on a number of factors in addition to race. Understanding how intersectionality works can make it much easier to relate to other people who are different than you.

What can you do:

Listen: Pay attention to how people identify themselves and listen to what they have to say about their identities.

Recognize difference: Understand that different people experience the world differently. A person with a disability has a much different view of the world than a marathon runner, for example. Our differences can also be our strengths, and shifting your perspective to

---

120   Coaston (2019); D'Cruz (2019); Kort (2020); "What Is Intersectionality, and What Does It Have to Do with Me?" (2017)

see the world through someone else's eyes can open your own eyes to different realities.

Avoid oversimplified language: Don't limit people to their identity labels. We are all much more complex than that.

Analyze the space you occupy: Do you hold space for others? Are you accommodating to people's different levels of need?

Seek other points of view: Try to be as broad-based and diverse in your interactions as possible. Meet a variety of different people, and listen to their points of view. You may not always agree, but you may gain a better understanding.

Show up: Be there for people when they need someone. Hold a door for the man in the wheelchair who is struggling to exit the building. Be an ear to someone who needs you to listen to them.

Help someone to know how their varying identities may be experienced as helping or hurting themselves or others. But remember that some people don't want to learn about their own intersectional identities. Respect that, and stop the conversation.

Oppressions, Violence, and Resistance are to a large extent determined by where a person falls on the identity wheel. For example, highly educated people may be more prone to doing anti-racist work, while an impoverished person may not have the resources to take the time out to lend a hand to the cause. Some people are more prone to being the victims of violent attacks, the elderly and infirm, for example.

We covered a lot of ground in this chapter, and hopefully you now have a better understanding of how systemic racism and microaggressions work, how to disarm them, how intersectionality works, and how to avoid some commonly used expressions that are racist in nature. It's a lot to take in at once, and some of these suggestions may not always be enough to disarm a microaggression or help you understand someone who's an enigma, or doesn't want to be understood, but it should give you a lot to think about even in terms of your own identity and behavior.

Chapter 9

How to Encourage Creativity and Build Self-Confidence in Your Child

A big part of successfully parenting a Black kid is nurturing their creativity and confidence and making sure they know how to self-advocate. In this chapter, we'll look at some of the best ways to make sure your child is growing into a strong, independent, and creative problem solver who thinks critically about the world around them. We'll also look at the problem of racism in the schools and what you and your child can do to combat it.

Support Your Child's Creativity

Ensuring your child has a creative outlet they can lean on will help them through difficult times. According to Dr. Aisha White, the director of the PRIDE (Positive Racial Identity Development in Early Education) Program at the University of Pittsburgh Office of Child Development, "Black art [...] can help children resist race-based negativity, giving them the strength, confidence and self-assurance that will help protect them from racial injustices for years to come."

Creative thinking and creative problem solving go hand in hand. If your child feels free to express themselves, they will spend less time internalizing negative messages they receive from elsewhere, and more time focusing on growth in the areas that are important building blocks to a happy life. Your child will need your support in this endeavor. Becoming a creative person doesn't just occur naturally, it requires nurturing and patience. Here are some tips to help you ensure they feel supported in exploring their creative side:[121]

Provide them with the tools they'll need to express themselves creatively. Give them a wide variety of media in which they can engage in self-expression. Things like crayons, finger paint, and colored pencils are a good start, but think outside the box too. Take your kids with you to the craft store and let them explore different arts and crafts. Let them tell you what they'd like to try, and do your best to help them. Talk to your kid about Black art, about Jacob Lawrence, Romare Bearden, Elizabeth Catlett, or Faith Ringgold. Contemporary artists like Kehinde Wiley also play an important part in depicting Black history through art, and the creativity they display can become a way to connect children of all ages to Black culture. Black artists can foster kids' pride toward their own culture and help them develop their self-esteem.

Designate an area in your home for creative expression. Make your home a laboratory for creativity. A special area designated for creativity will help keep down the mess that often comes with creative expression and will also give your child a feeling of being valued. Put on display illustrations by Black artists like Kadir Nelson, Don Tate, and Vashti Harrison whose work takes an intentional, in-your-face stance that says all black is beautiful, giving parents the opportunity to discuss colors with all ages, in a context that celebrates things that are dark. In a world that is filled with hate, anger, racism and violence,

---

121 Carter (2008); Tartakovsky (2018)

all kids need them to have a safe and secure place, and creativity can become that space. Later in life, kids who have learned to express their creativity become an integral part of the Black movement and use art to channel their energies. Think about Naomi Osaka, for instance, using her masks as a creative way to protest. Think about Toni Morrison's powerful poetry, the great strength and texture of her stories about Black identity.

Think about Augusta Savage, a Black art teacher and sculptor who helped Shape the Harlem Renaissance. Surround your children with art and beauty throughout their lives so they learn to communicate openly and honestly and to use their own incredible talent to express the entire spectrum of their emotions.

Encourage your kids to read for fun and participate in the arts. All children love seeing faces like theirs within the pages of their picture books. While for many years it could be challenging to find books that (positively) featured Black characters, there has fortunately been a large increase in the number of "diverse" books published in recent years—books that build confidence and instill pride in young Black readers, and counter negative messages that children may be absorbing from other media outlets. Start by reading to your kids when they are little and take them to different arts events so that when they are older, they'll want to read for fun and participate in the arts. If you have a teenager, explore modern Black music with them, or plan some time to watch powerful Black films together and discover Black filmmakers like Issa Rae who became the first Black woman to create and star in a premium cable series (she is the creator and star of HBO's hit series, *Insecure*) or Ava DuVernay who became the first Black woman to direct a film nominated for a Best Picture Oscar—*Selma*—and is also the first Black female director to win the director's prize at the Sundance Film Festival in 2012.

Appreciating and understanding Black literature and Black art will not only give your child a richer art education, but it will also help them understand Black culture, Black history, and the serious race and social justice issues Black people are facing right now.

Keep it simple. Especially in the beginning, there's no need to spend a lot of money on creative supplies. Not everyone can afford a grand piano, but an electronic keyboard may be within reach. For visual arts, you can recycle brown paper bags into a canvas for coloring or painting, for example. Teacher Tanya Merriman suggests modeling the art of abstract expressionist Alma Thomas with torn paper collages or using the work of Aaron Douglas to show children how to really look at art; kids can also choose an important moment or series of moments from their personal and family history and visually represent it, using one of Jacob Lawrence's palettes. (All these artists are easily Googleable and there are family-friendly activities suitable for all ages.) Artistic activities will allow your child the opportunity to express "divergent thought." Divergent thought is a creative way of thinking where nonlinear ideas are expressed quickly. It's similar to brainstorming. Divergent thinkers can find many different solutions to problems.

Let your kids have some "free time." Nowadays parents have a tendency to overschedule activities for their kids. Instead, let them have some free time where they can engage in activities of their choosing. If you've taught them well and diversified their media intake by including more Black musicians in their daily music jams, your small kids might choose to spend time with Uncle Devin, a singer who uses percussion instruments to take kids on a musical journey with impacting life lessons. They might show appreciation for Ella Jenkins, the legendary children's folk singer, or Culture Queen's affirmations and upbeat music meant to help boost your child's confidence. Teenagers might enjoy the list of powerful Black songs I curated in my young-adult book, *Badass Black Girl.* Don't micromanage. Let your kids have the freedom to choose their own activities. Give them the autonomy to explore what they want to do. You don't have to be bossy all the time.

Make it a sensory experience. Activating all of your child's senses helps them to fully engage in the activity. Along with sight and smell, find activities that involve hearing, taste, and touch. Get down in the dirt with them and make some mud pies! Let your kids get dirty; allow for uninhibited play by letting them make a mess. (Kids usually clean up nice with soap and water.) Listen to music, and introduce your child (whatever their age) to songs that speak to the Black experience and elicit a deep sense of pride and self-worth, including Nina Simone's "Young, Gifted, and Black," Jaheim's "Fabulous," James Brown's "Say It Loud: I'm Black and Proud," Stevie Wonder's "Black Man," Black Star's "Brown Skin Lady," Angie Stone's "Brotha," Mos Def's "Umi Say," Deniece Williams's "Black Butterfly," James Weldon Johnson's "Lift Every Voice and Sing," and Donny Hathaway's "Someday We'll All Be Free."

Talk about creativity. Make creativity a part of your daily discussions. Talk about the way everyday creative projects—including the braiding of our Black hair or the art involved in making yams and collard greens—are cultural ties that bind us to our ancestral home, Africa. Help your child connect the dots of our heritage and legacy. For this, you need to keep the conversation going: Ask your child what they did today that was creative and fun; ask them to think critically about news items or things they see in the media; brainstorm creative solutions with your kids, challenging them to come up with different solutions to the same problem. Parents are key in nurturing creative problem solving and critical thinking skills.

Help your children find and pursue their passions. Pay close attention to what comes naturally to your kids and makes them happy. Encourage them to do the things they are passionate about, whether it's writing or painting or playing a musical instrument or something else entirely; dancing or rapping can become an outlet for confidence and fighting prejudice, and they can easily channel a talent for painting into an education about Black artists. But be careful: Don't care so much for what your kids achieve. They don't have to be the best at everything they do. Allow them to try and fail and try again or try something else entirely. Learning to lose gracefully is an important lesson. Also, don't reward children for exhibiting creativity. Give praise when it's warranted for something special your children create, but make creativity an expectation with rewards and benefits of its own.

Take time for your own creativity. Let your kids see you being creative yourself. Explore different avenues for your own creative expression, and share that with your children. You're their first role model, and they'll learn to be creative if they see you engaging in your own art.

Creativity isn't just about arts and crafts. It's a way of life. There are several benefits to engaging your children in creativity. It leads to creative problem solving, reduces stress and anxiety, encourages innovation and leads to feelings of pride and accomplishment, to name just a few of the many ways creativity is good for your kids. Besides those, it's just plain fun. Along with instilling creativity, you'll want to foster self-confidence in your children.

How to Encourage Confidence

Raising a confident Black child is a challenge because so much of the way systemic racism works is by undermining Black people's sense of self-worth and achievement. You may find that encouraging confidence is a daily struggle for you and for your kids, especially if they've been bullied or picked on. Keep trying to encourage their confidence anyway. Here are some tips for building self-confidence in your child:[122]

Make sure your kids know that your love is unconditional. Don't withhold love if they do something differently than you would like; let them know you'll love them no matter what. This applies to all parents, but it's particularly important for a Black child: Make sure you fill them with the love the world around them won't always provide, do your best to let them know they are beautiful, loved and, most importantly, free. Give them lots of hugs; showing your kids affection lets them know you care about them. Tell them you love them frequently, but also show them by listening to them, valuing their opinions and making sure they have some alone, one-on-one time with you when you can give them undivided attention.

Make dates with them to do fun things that you both enjoy, and practice positive self-talk; this might seem a little awkward at first, but when you hear them say something like, "I'm so stupid," stop them and encourage them to talk positively to and about themselves. (This is so, so important. Have you seen the viral video posted by Shabria Redmond, an Atlanta-based hairdresser and rapper, of the little girl who was getting her hair done and said she was ugly? That was heartbreaking.) If you're raising a teenage girl, I recommend you get them the book *Black Girl Affirmations: Words of Resilience from Radical Black Women.*

Praise your child the right way. Praise them in a way that acknowledges their choices and actions. Tell them, "I like the way you blocked that goal," not, "You are the best goalie who ever lived!" Let them overhear you saying positive things about them to other people; don't brag, but do mention notable achievements to other people within earshot of your children. Create a "Wall of Fame" in your house to celebrate their achievements. Hang certificates and medals,

---

122   See References: How to Encourage Confidence

and display trophies in a special spot designated just for them. Hang their artwork or portraits in your house; this will give your children a sense of belonging. Resist the urge to compare them to others: See each of your children as an individual with their own set of positive attributes and shortcomings. In fact, address them by their name. This lets them feel like you really see and hear them and appreciate them for who they are as an individual. Teach them to have pride in their name, especially when this country diminishes their value because they're named Jamal or LaQuisha.[123] Teach them about the history of Black names and their relationship to the development of Black culture, so that they don't feel diminished by society. Black names signify strength and a voice. Black names have power!

Don't be intimidated by your child's emotions. It is especially important for Black kids to know they're allowed to feel sad and cry, and they should be encouraged to open up about these feelings. I know we toughen our children because we know how cruel the world can be, we encourage them to eat their feelings a lot (see Chris Rock's stand up titled "Tambourine"), but feelings get hurt, it's a part of life, and I suggest letting your child feel whatever comes naturally. Encourage them to connect with their emotions and express their feelings by asking, "How does that make you feel?" In addition to raising their level of assertiveness, this will help build an honest, open relationship between the two of you. On the flip side, however, don't let on that you're worried about them. If they are in danger, by all means say so ("Let's talk about police encounters"), but don't allow your worries about the world to prevent your child from being a child. If they upset you, let them understand you are upset with the choices they made, not with them as a person. Criticize the choices, not the person making them.

123 Howard (2020)

Allow them to act their age. This is especially important for Black children who are subject to adultification. Let your two-year-old throw a temper tantrum, for example. It's normal. Give them age-appropriate chores around the house. Starting when they are very young, children get a feeling of self-accomplishment from completing tasks; it also helps them feel like they are contributing to the household and they learn to be self-sufficient. Even something as simple as pouring the cheesy ham and hash brown mix into the baking pan can give a kid a feeling of accomplishment. Offering your child options is empowering: it makes them feel like they have a say in what happens to them. Don't set your child up for failure: If you know that a task is too big of a challenge for your kid, offer to help them complete the task, or be ready to step in if it gets to be too much for them. Avoid shortcuts or easy ways out, though. Resist the temptation to make a task too easy for your child. If you give them a challenge, chances are they will rise to meet it.

Foster curiosity. Allow your kids to use their imagination in play; let them make up new rules for games and play along. Encourage your child to ask lots of questions about everything, even when these questions make you uncomfortable ("Why are some police unfair to Black people?" "Why are people saying, 'Black Lives Matter' instead of 'all lives matter'?" "What does 'dead' mean?") or you don't know the answer ("How do I become a hippotherapist?"). Keep your eyes and ears open for opportunities for your kids and help them find new experiences and try new things. Encourage them to try a public speaking club (like Toastmasters) for example, or theater, where they can gain the confidence to face a crowd on their own while also learning about great contemporary Black playwrights like Jocelyn Bioh, Francisca Da Silveria, Marcus Gardley, Branden Jacobs-Jenkins, Adrienne Kennedy, Tarell Alvin McCraney, Antoinette Nwandu, Robert O'Hara, Dael Orlandersmith, and Mfonsio Udofia.

Teach them what you know, maybe wood shopping, sculpting, or quilting, and any other skill set with ancestral significance. Be patient and celebrate learning as something exciting and fun! Acknowledge how hard it is to step out of one's comfort zone and applaud your child when they are brave and try something new. Even if they don't stick with learning a new skill, encourage them to try different things.

Present them with new challenges. Present them with simple problems you are facing ("I can never find my keys") and ask them what they would do. Ask them for their opinion or advice, and really listen to what they say. Finding their own solutions fosters your child's self-reliance, an important aspect of self-confidence. If your child is stuck, offer to help them brainstorm, but let them find the solution on their own. Offer help and support, but not too much. Give them just enough help to get over any impasse they might be facing, and let them know you believe in their ability to do whatever task they are attempting. Win or lose, appreciate the effort: Show your kid you noticed how much they tried even if they didn't win in the end; instead of criticizing their performance, ask instead how they felt about it, and be prepared to listen. Ask them how they would do it differently next time, and if possible, encourage them to try again; this will help them see mistakes as a means of learning. Give them praise when they face an adverse situation: Let them know you see them struggling, and that it's good for them to keep trying. Competence at any skill is achieved through lots and lots of practice. Even if it can be painful to listen to an hour of trumpet practice every night, encourage your kids to put in the practice time.

Be authoritative, but not too strict or forceful. Black parents are under a lot of pressure to instill fear and demand the respect of their children. But as someone who's worked in youth development, fighting for Black children to be treated with dignity and respect, I can tell you that "tough love" is in direct conflict with the values of equity and justice. The key is to be an authority without resorting to dictatorship. Be flexible, but firm. Stop controlling and start coaching. Be a good coach, and encourage your kids, not a "bad coach" who is overly critical and bossy. Every consequence given should match the offense, and I suggest focusing on requiring the child to think before and after they act. Teach a child why you deem something wrong or right rather than just beat and punish them. Teach them about impact, and let them know they can have an impact on the outside world. Show them that little things (helping an elderly neighbor with their groceries, for example) make positive changes in their environment.

Teach them how to set and achieve goals. Break it down step by step with them so they see goal-making as a process. Say, for example, your child has a hard time cleaning up their messes. Rather than telling the child he or she is a mess, help them see how they can break the clean-up down into steps and offer them an incentive to complete each task. For example, "Once you get all of your dirty clothes in the hamper, we can watch _____" or [another reward you know the child will work for]. This way the child begins to feel less overwhelmed and more personally empowered. This goes for all age groups, but is especially important once your child starts completing tasks on their own.

The best way to build self-esteem in a child is through positive reinforcement. If your child completes a goal or learns a new skill, give them plenty of praise, "That's great! I'm proud of you! I knew you could do it!" Remember perfection is not a goal. Let your kids know it's okay to mess things up and that you don't expect them to be perfect every time they try something. Embrace imperfections. Try to see imperfection as an expression of individuality. There is something genuinely unique in the mistakes we make. Appreciate that uniqueness. Allow kids to fail. But let them see failure as a way to learn.

Work on improving your own confidence. Before you even begin looking for ways to build your child's self-esteem, consider how you feel about yourself. How healthy is your self-esteem? Parents model just about everything for their kids, including feelings of self-worth. If your self-esteem is low, ask yourself why, and start to strategize ways you can boost it. No one is perfect. We all have flaws, but understanding that if you are weak in some areas, you probably possess strengths in others will help bring some balance into your sense of self. It is important that you watch yourself when talking to your kids. If you say things like, "I'm so stupid," your kids will pick up on that and mimic it in their own internal dialogues. Your child needs you to model positive self-talk.

Your internal dialogue is a big part of what makes up your sense of self. And if your inner dialogue is beating you up every day, it's likely you'll pass that along to your kids. Start looking for solutions instead of obsessing about mistakes. Say you repeatedly get a parking ticket at a place you visit regularly. Rather than telling yourself that you're a failure, start putting a roll of quarters in the car so you can pay the parking meter, and praise yourself when you remember to pay the meter. Simple steps like that will help you build self-esteem a little at a time.

You're your child's role model, and they look to you to see how they should treat themselves. In general, make sure they are surrounded by positive, confident people. Help them choose friends who are positive and confident also.

The biggest part of fostering confidence in your children is letting them do things on their own and succeed or fail at it. This gives them a feeling of accomplishment and empowerment or teaches them to try another approach. An empowered child is more likely to be a happy child, and even failure has its own rewards. An empowered child has a good healthy sense of sense and is less likely to be bullied or to internalize racism and insults.

Self-Esteem and Confidence by Age Group

In this next section, I break down different ways you can work with your child to foster a healthy sense of self-esteem. It's broken down by age group to help you more easily access the activities and my suggestions for your particular child. Some of these are things I've mentioned already, but they bear repeating. I've included some resources for you and your kids that I think may be helpful, also broken down by age group.

Zero to three years of age

One would think there is little to be done to build self-esteem in infants and very young toddlers, but you are setting the stage for when they are older and their sense of self may be under attack by the culture of racism. Start giving praise when your child reaches milestones like learning to stand on their own, hold their own bottle, or feed themselves.

Some other things you can do:

- Read positive and affirming books and watch positive and affirming children's programming with your baby. This includes reading *Beautiful, Beautiful Me,* by Ashley Sirah Hinton (illustrated by Vanessa Brantley), watching "I Love My Hair" from Sesame Street, and listening to *Talking Race with Young Children*, a podcast from NPR.

- Give them praise for accomplishing even the simplest tasks like feeding themselves.

- Engage in play with your child that gives them an opportunity to meet goals and receive praise. For example, turn picking up the toys at the end of play time into a game. When your child puts a toy away, give them praise. (By the way, I highly recommend a plush basket of "snuggly dolls" with a range of skin tones for this age.)

- Let them hear you say kind things to other people. Even if they are still learning to talk, your tone of voice is communicating clear messages to them.

- Involve them in play groups with a diverse range of children and praise them for playing nicely. If they misbehave, rather than telling them they were bad, calmly remove them from the play area temporarily and tell them how they should behave. "We don't hit people. We are gentle with other people." When they return, if the behavior changes, praise them. "That's nice!"

Three to eleven years old

Building self-esteem in toddlers and kindergarten aged children requires patience, because of the number of temper tantrums children this age tend to throw. Stay calm, and don't feed into any tantrums by telling the child they are bad. Instead, give them something to look forward to once the tantrum has passed. "When you're done throwing the tantrum, we can read this book, or play with blocks, but we can play when you are this upset." Let them throw their tantrum, and when they are done, try to discuss it with them, "Why were you so upset?" Often it won't make a lot of sense. They are toddlers after all. As your child grows into their elementary school age years, the talks you have about self-esteem will become more crucial as this is the stage when bullying starts and they will be able to handle that challenge more easily if they have a solid sense of identity at this stage.

- At this age, children can start completing chores like feeding pets. You'll need to supervise, but it will give them a sense of accomplishment.

- Kids this age are starting school, if you find they are getting frustrated with their schoolwork, see if you can break it down into steps to make it easier for them. When choosing supplemental materials, be sure to choose those that embrace diversity. For example, watch *CNN and Sesame Street Town Hall: Standing Up to Racism*. Also available on YouTube: *Systemic Racism Explained*. Listen to a reading of *We're Different, We're the Same* by Bobbi Jane Kates. When you play with your child, select the Crayola skin color crayon packs and Speedy Kids coloring books as they celebrate different skin colors. Buy games and puzzles featuring children from a variety of cultures (The Barefoot Kids books come to mind).

- Praise them frequently when they take the initiative to do something kind for others. If they pick you a bouquet of weeds from the garden, thank them, and put them in a vase where you can look at them.

- While appearance is the least important part of self-esteem, in a Black child, praising Blackness will set up a foundation for later when they may be criticized for their hair or skin color. Teach them to love their hair and skin. Watch affirming video programs on television where all the kids are beautiful, but also find programs like *Good Hair,* and *Hair Love* and books like *Sulwe* by Lupita Nyong'o and *I Like Myself* by Karen Beaumont where the focus is on affirming Black love. If they have questions about Blackness and racism, other books to read with your child include *A Kids Book About Racism* by Jelani Memory or *Something Happened in Our Town: A Child's Story About Racial Injustice*, by Marianne Celano, Marietta Collins, and Ann Hazzard. The Brown Bookshelf promotes African American children's book authors and illustrators, and Embrace Race (a community and advocacy site for parents) has listed thirty-one children's books to support conversations on race, racism, and resistance. Common Sense Media has curated a list of eighty books with diverse, multicultural characters for preschoolers and older, some of which could easily be suitable for babies and toddlers.

- Start listening to what your child is saying about themselves and correct them if you hear negative self-talk. If, for example they say, "I am stupid," ask them why they would say such a thing. Oftentimes it's just frustration over something they are struggling to do on their own. Show them how to complete the task and walk it through with them.

- Be a role model for your kids. Discuss your own strengths and weaknesses with your kids. Maybe you had a hard time with math when you were in school. How did you work to overcome the problem? Let your kids know everyone faces challenges.

- Teach them about natural consequences. Rather than punishment, let them face the consequences of their actions, good or bad. For example, if they need to clean their room, set a positive reinforcement. "If you clean your room, you can play video games." Talk about how to break that goal into tasks. For example, "pick up your dirty clothes, make the bed, sweep the floor." And then leave them to complete the task. If they complete it, they earn the positive reinforcement. If not, then the natural consequence of not cleaning is no video games. More often, children will rise to a challenge.

- Provide clear, but critical feedback, set attainable goals. "I see you got a D in English this semester. Let's talk about how that happened. Do you think if we worked on your homework every night, we could get that grade up to a B next term?"

- Have a growth mindset that is tied to increasing independence. Say your child wants to learn to ride a bike. Let them fall often. You can push them around the neighborhood for so long, but eventually you have to let go and let them find balance. The same thing goes for other goals they are trying to meet. If you are teaching them to do the dishes for example, show them a couple of times, but then let them try it on their own. You can point out where they need to do a better job, but explain it's just part of the process of learning a new skill.

- Praise your child's efforts, not just the end results.

- Encourage extracurricular activities and mentors. Find your child's area of strength. If they are good at bowling, help them find a bowling league in their age group. If they like singing, find them a choir where they can be with others who share the same talents.

- Know your child's teachers and mentors. Have regular discussions with the other adults in your child's life to make sure they are being affirmed outside of the home. If your child is running into trouble at school, ask the teacher how they can improve, and how you can help them.

- Continue to monitor your child's self-talk. How are they talking about themselves? If you hear them saying negative things about themselves, ask them why. Discuss ways they could shift the dialogue to be more positive and self-affirming. Practice saying affirmations with them in front of the bathroom mirror like, "I love my Black skin. I love my curly/kinky hair. I am Black and beautiful. I am intelligent." There is a reason why Black parents should spend time in front of the mirror repeating affirmations with their children: Racism is tough at that age because your child's classmates begin to show more love to white girls, for example, than Black girls. Black girls are seen as nasty and confrontational to their teachers; their opinions and knowledge can be mocked or belittled. Use affirmations as a tool to help your child believe in their worth as a Black child. Chapter 10, about self-advocacy, will provide you with tips on how to handle racism in teachers, in peers, in administration, in authority figures who tell your child, for example, that their paper was plagiarized, that their hair needs to follow school rules, that they are disrespectful for correcting the teacher, etc.

- Send your child love notes and let them know they make you proud. Maybe not every day, but once in a while, surprise them by letting them know you think they are beautiful and strong and smart.

Eleven and up

If you have been working on building self-esteem in your child up to this age, it should get easier from here. Kids by this point should understand that mistakes are a learning opportunity and that everyone runs into rough spots.

- Continue to monitor your child's self-talk. Make sure you tell them positive things also.

- Teach your child about personal affirmations for when they run into self-doubt or self-pity. Phrases like, "I am strong," "I am unique," and "I can make a difference."

- Kids at this age crave independence. Praise them when they accomplish goals they set for themselves, and give them the room to make mistakes.

- Introduce them to role models from history, and trailblazers they can look up to and be inspired by (we'll discuss this further in the next chapter). Let them know they can be as great as they choose to become. Let them know you are proud of their accomplishments.

- Continue to have discussions with your child's teachers and role models. Check in and see how they are doing.

- Know your child's friends and their parents. If your child is spending time at other children's homes, take the time to meet the children and their parents. Give the parents your contact information if there are any problems you should know about.

- Continue to encourage extracurricular activities and
  sports involvement.

Building self-esteem is an ongoing process. Never miss the chance to
let your kid know you think they are great just the way they are. Your
child will appreciate knowing that you hold them in high regard,
and it will help foster the kind of strength of character they'll need to
remain strong and healthy as they grow.

Chapter 10

How to Teach Your Child to Self-Advocate

What is self-advocacy?

Put simply, self-advocacy is the ability to speak for oneself. It also involves making decisions that will impact one's life, understanding rights and responsibilities, creative problem solving, listening and learning, asking for help, and becoming self-determined.[124]

Why is it important for your child to learn to self-advocate? Because you won't always be there to speak up for them. Learning to self-advocate will give them knowledge they will need to succeed in life and allow them to participate in decision-making about their future. This is especially important for Black schoolchildren who are often undervalued and under-challenged by the public-school system.

Learning to Self-Advocate will Teach Your Children to:

1. **Believe in themselves.** A child who knows how to successfully self-advocate becomes confident in their ability to make decisions about their own life and is empowered.

2.   **Know their rights.** A child who knows their rights is less likely to have their rights taken away.

3.   **Get the facts.** A child who understands how to self-advocate is able to gather information and listen to the other side.

4.   **Plan a strategy.** A child who knows how to self-advocate can make a plan to ensure their decisions are respected.

5.   **Gather support.** Your child may lean on you for support, but successfully knowing how to self-advocate often involves locating mentors or supportive people outside the family unit.

6.   **Target efforts.** Teaching your children to self-advocate helps them understand who they need to speak to when they need to communicate about an issue important to them.

7.   **Express themselves clearly and assertively.** By teaching your child to self-advocate, you teach them how to clearly articulate their needs. A child who knows how to self-advocate is assertive without being domineering and can clearly state their needs.

8.   **Be Firm and persistent.** A self-advocating child knows how to remain steadfast in the face of adversity and remain rooted in their challenge to authority.

School is the place where your child will likely have the most need to self-advocate. Whether it is calling a teacher out for implicit bias or petitioning to take advanced courses, your child will need to know how to speak for themselves. Here are some suggestions for how to prepare your child to self-advocate at school:

Create awareness. Have a running dialogue about learning differences. Point out to your child the different ways people learn. Make sure they understand that differences are just differences; they aren't necessarily hierarchical. Discuss your child's strengths and weak points with them. Maybe your kid is a whiz at math but has a harder time with language arts. Make sure they are aware of their own strengths and weaknesses and that they take a role in planning their education.

Promote decision-making. Let your children pick their own classes if they are in middle or high school. Make sure your child knows they have the biggest say in decisions about school that affect them. Support their choices. Let them know they have your support, but that you are willing to give an opinion if they need to make a choice. If your child has an Individualized Education Plan (IEP), encourage them to be involved in any meetings. If they don't have an IEP, make sure they know that they are responsible for coordinating regular student reviews with their teacher.

Encourage your child to ask for help. Many children are afraid to ask for help when they need it; let your child know that asking for assistance if they are overwhelmed is a positive thing. Your child should see self-advocacy as a positive skill, not one to be ashamed of, so praise your child when they make an effort to state their needs. Let them know you are proud of them when they do speak up. Together, practice ways to talk to teachers about their issues. Role play different scenarios with your child so they are prepared to self-advocate. If needed, make sure your child knows they can use classroom accommodations for special needs. Or talk to them about other accommodations that are available to all students. If an issue arises, let your child try to solve it first before you intervene. This empowers your child to be self-determined.

Pair them up with a mentor. Help your child find a role model or a mentor. Find someone your child clicks with that they can rely on for support in the school like a guidance counselor or teacher. Encourage them to get a job or volunteer, and encourage them to think about their future. Ask them where they want to be in five years, ten years. What do they want to study in college?

Teach your child what their rights are and how to exercise them. Make sure they approach the idea of rights from a positive standpoint, and never hesitate to discuss self-advocacy. There may be times during their school years when they have to deal with racism in the classroom on their own, and this is good practice for when they reach the age of maturity. But having this talk should be a positive experience for both of you. Remember, you are empowering them to make choices about their own life.

What to say:

1. "Remember the only person who is an expert on YOU is YOU."

2. "Approach the person you are talking to with respect. You are more likely to earn respect in this way."

3. "Be direct. Get to the point quickly."

4. "You can always come to me for help if you get overwhelmed."

5. "You don't always have to be right. More often, you will be partially right, and the other person may have an important point you didn't understand."

6. "I believe in you. You have all the tools you need to advocate for yourself."

Racism in the Schools

How Racism Affects Black Children in Public schools

There is a preponderance of evidence that proves racism in the schools is a systemic reality. A number of studies have been done that show it is a major problem that fuels the school-to-prison pipeline.[125]

Here are some of the startling facts about racism in the schools that you should be aware of:

- Black students are three times more likely to be suspended or expelled as white students.

- A 2015 report from the University of Pennsylvania Center for the Study of Race and Equity in Education found that just thirteen Southern states (Alabama, Arkansas, Florida, Georgia, Kentucky, Louisiana, Mississippi, North Carolina, South Carolina, Tennessee, Texas, Virginia, and West Virginia) reported 50 percent of Black suspensions from school and 55 percent of Black student expulsions.

- Another study found that in eighty-four Southern school districts, 100 percent of the students suspended were Black.

- Black Students make up 18 percent of the preschool population, but were suspended 50 percent of the time.

- Yet another study found that Black boys start to be considered threatening at about the age of five years.

- High suspension rates among Black students leads to higher absenteeism and more contact with the criminal justice system.

- Black students are more likely to attend schools with a higher police presence on campus which puts them in more contact with the criminal justice system.

---

125   See References: Chapter 10, Racism in the Schools

- Black students are half as likely as white students to participate in programs for gifted and/or talented students.

- A 2015 study found that Black, Native American, and Hispanic children in Washington were far less likely to have qualified teachers. Their teachers tended to have the least classroom experience, the lowest licensing exam scores, and the poorest track records of improving student test scores.

For a key to understanding systemic racism, just look at our schools.

There are many problems in the public-school system in regard to racism, perhaps the biggest is the lack of educators who are brown or Black. Studies have shown that Black students are more likely to sign up for gifted or advanced placement classes if they are taught by an educator of color. However, hiring practices are subject to implicit bias, and Black teachers are less likely to be hired. And if they are hired, they are less likely to receive a comparable salary to their white peers.

With a lack of Black educators in the classroom, implicit bias is more likely to occur, and studies show this is the case. White teachers are more likely to assess Black students less favorably than white students even if their test scores are identical. Black students are far more likely to go through school without ever having a teacher of color. And because they don't see themselves represented in the teaching profession, they are less likely to attend college programs for teachers if they go to college at all. The cost of college programs and teacher exams is cost prohibitive to many students of color.

To further complicate matters, schools are more segregated now than they were in the 1970s when bussing programs became popular. This means that Black students are more likely to attend schools in poor neighborhoods and the schools there have fewer resources than schools in more affluent neighborhoods.

What does all this mean for your child?

Your Black child is facing obstacles to their success as an adult the minute they enter kindergarten. The system is geared toward making it harder for them to achieve the same kind of education as their non-Black peers. They need to learn to advocate for themselves, and they need you to have their back too. It's also important that you look for anti-racist teachers your children can work with who understand the limitations they are facing.

For Afro-Caribbean and Afro-Latinx kids, language differences might bring them an extra level of scrutiny. Maybe your child speaks with an accent, for example. In addition to being Black, they are "foreign." They might feel embarrassed and "othered" if (in addition to their beautiful Black skin, Black hair, and other Black features they inherited from their African ancestors) you haven't taught them to embrace with pride the languages they speak at home.

How Anti-racist Teachers Operate[126]

- They see the success of their Black students as a measure of their success as educators.

- They encourage their Black students to excel in coursework.

- They make themselves available to Black students for after class discussions.

- They don't tolerate bullying or racist classroom misbehavior from non-Black students.

- They grade fairly.

- They study pedagogy that values the Black experience and they decolonize teaching.

- They analyze their approaches to teaching to make sure they reach all of their students.

---

126 McKamey (2020)

- They incorporate oral presentations for students who may not speak or write Standard English.

- They listen to Black parents' concerns about their children.

How to Root out Anti-Black Racism in Your Child's School

It is possible to root out anti-Black racism in the school system, but it takes a concerted effort and the cooperation of school administrators.[127] Here are a few of the ways to root out anti-Black racism in the school where your child goes:

1. **Call it what it is.** If your child is the object of racist bullying by other students, or worse, by a teacher, name it as racism and provide clear examples of racist behavior to the administration at the school. Document everything.

2. **Believe your child.** Part of why the #MeToo movement was successful is that people believed the women who gave witness to sexual harassment and abuse. There is a tendency not to believe a Black student when they report implicit bias or racism. Believe them, help them advocate for themselves and support them in their efforts to get an equal education. Ask questions about your child's experience in school.

3. **Consistently show your child models of Black excellence.** So much of education is centered on "Black inferiority" that it is hard to find examples of Black intellectual excellence in the classroom. Make sure your child has Black intellectual role models, whether they come from media or real-life examples. Refuse to settle for any teacher who insists your child is destined to mediocrity because of the color of their skin.

4. **Show up for your child.** Be in their corner and go all out to show them you will not allow them to be treated poorly. Showing up for your child will require that you stay informed:

---

127 Howard (2020)

research ways to get what you want from a parent-teacher conference, and effectively confront an administration that shrugs you off, for example. What do you do when regional directors give you the runaround? How do you use the local media in the case of a serious racist incident? Be prepared!

You want your child to be able to stand up for themselves, but keep in mind, they may need you to help advocate for them. Even the best teachers make mistakes, and they may miss something you understand about your own child and their learning style. So be ready to step in and help your kid out if it gets overwhelming.

Parenting a Black Child: A Labor of Love

When you first became a parent to a Black child, chances are, all the repercussions and concerns you'd face as they grew weren't in the forefront of your mind. Making sure you got enough rest, and that your infant was eating, taking all of the photos of every milestone, delighting in tiny fingers and toes, and being smitten by the music of their first giggles were the things that occupied your attention, and it should be that way for new parents, but it gets a lot more complicated when your child is Black. The concerns are everywhere and can fill your days with worry. Momfully.you x@Happyasamother created an infographic that clearly lays out the kinds of things parents of Black kids have to worry about. They include:

- Protecting their childhood innocence
- Convincing the world of their worth
- Teaching them how to respond to racism
- Choosing daycares and schools that have representation
- Fearing for their safety because of their skin color
- Educating them on their history

- Worrying about unequal opportunities
- Worrying about their child being perceived as a threat
- Making sure they have Black and brown friends
- Teaching them to love their skin and hair
- Inspiring them to break stereotypes
- Feeling pressure to have well-behaved children

The sad truth is that being Black is stressful on its own. Being a parent to a Black child carries an additional weight of stress, and it's important that you take time out of your day to recognize this fact and take care of yourself so that you remain healthy and are able to parent your child in the ways they need you.

Together, we're going to look at the mental and physical tolls of racism with your child's health in mind, but remember you matter too, and all of the stressors your child is feeling are ones that affect you as well. The strategies I suggest for helping your child relieve stress are ones you should consider for yourself to prevent burnout and illness. Remember, before you can take care of anyone else, you need to make sure you're taking care of yourself.

Health Impact of Racism

We've gone over how to talk to your kids about racism, but the sad truth is that you cannot protect your children from racist incidents outside the home. Even if your child never experiences a racist encounter directly, they are likely to see one of the many videos online of Black men and women being killed violently—and that will likely affect them. Even witnessing racism second hand has a tremendous impact on a child and can lead to a host of physical and mental health issues. Racism is a socially transmitted illness that should be a major public health concern.[128] But it's often not seen as such.

To further complicate the problem of racism and health, Black people are less likely to have adequate access to medical care or are poorly/under treated when they do seek help. They may have trouble locating a healthcare professional with cultural sensitivity to the issues your child is struggling with. Lack of adequate insurance can be a barrier for many people who need help but cannot afford it. In some communities, including Afro-Latinx and Afro-Caribbean communities, there may be a language barrier. There is also a pervasive stigma among many Black people associated with seeking help for mental illnesses or discussing painful emotions, so even if a problem is identified, it can go untreated.

The Physical Toll of Racism

The constant stress of racism triggers a response in your adrenal glands which releases stress hormones including cortisol. Increased cortisol levels in your blood has been linked to:

- Insomnia
- Autoimmune diseases
- Heart disease
- High blood pressure
- Diabetes
- Obesity
- Weakened immune response
- Gastrointestinal disorders
- Respiratory infections
- Inflammatory conditions

---

128   See References: Chapter 10: Health Impact of Racism

The Mental Toll of Racism

The effect of all that stress on the body affects the mind as well. Suicide rates are higher among Black teens than any other group. Depression and anxiety are common after-effects of racism, along with racial trauma, which manifests similarly to post-traumatic stress disorder.[129]

Early warning signs of racial trauma include:

- Body aches
- Fatigue
- Anxiety
- Depression
- Difficulty sleeping

In the acute stage of racial trauma, the symptoms progress to the point that they interfere with a person's ability to work or attend school. Signs of acute racial trauma include:

- Hypervigilance
- Heightened emotional states
- Depression
- Anxiety
- Persistent intrusive memories or thoughts
- Lack of appetite
- Increased startle response
- Physical exhaustion
- Self-destructive behaviors such as drug or alcohol abuse or careless risk-taking

---

129   See References: Chapter 10, The Mental Toll of Racism

- Migraines

- Outbursts of anger

- Nightmares

- Emotional numbness

- Difficulty concentrating

- Flashbacks

- Avoidant behaviors or dissociation

- Mental exhaustion

Black Kids and Suicide

The chronic stress of dealing with racism can have another tragic effect, an increase in suicide rates among Black youth. Suicide is the second highest leading cause of death among all adolescents across every ethnic group after accidents, but the trends for Black youth are especially disturbing. A 2019 study in the journal *Pediatrics* found that self-reported suicide attempts rose 73 percent among Black adolescents between 1997 and 2017, but fell 7.5 percent among white adolescents during the same timeframe.[130]

Fifteen-year-old Torian Williams was an honor school student, played basketball and the saxophone, and sang in his church choir, and by all appearances seemed to be an average young man with a bright future ahead of him when his mother Kathy came home and found he had shot himself to death with his stepfather's police revolver. "I did not know that Torian was probably depressed or even thinking about taking his life," she said. "None of us knew it. None of his friends. He just had all of these wonderful things going on in his life."[131]

---

130   Lindsey (2017)

131   Runcie (2019)

What Kathy Williams may not have realized is that suicidal attempts are often an impulsive action carried out without a lot of planning, but Black boys, even those as young as five to eleven years old, are more likely to use more fatal means in their attempt.

The rise in suicides among Black youth can be attributed to several factors including an increased internalization of racism and bullying, a decline in the coping mechanisms available, and a lack of psychiatric intervention or treatment. Research shows that the rise in suicides among Black boys is often related to the punitive environment of schools for Black children.

Black girls seem to experience more stress from cyberbullying and interpersonal interactions on social media. The same *Pediatrics* study found that Black girls reported more feelings of hopelessness and depression, which can lead to an increase in suicidal ideation. In 2007, 36 percent of Black girls reported those feelings, but by 2017, the number reporting had risen to greater than 41 percent.

Be on the lookout for the signs of depression

The constant barrage of outright racism from classmates, implicit bias from educators, and microaggressions that students face can leave them traumatized if it's unchecked. It is critical that parents of Black children be on the lookout for signs of depression, which include physical complaints (headaches, stomach aches, etc.), loss of appetite, irritability, anger, and sleep disturbances, to name a few. If your child is depressed, it is imperative that you seek immediate medical help.

In Afro-Caribbean communities, anti-Black racism, and other forms of systemic oppression, can break our young people too, and the fact that mental health is still taboo in many families puts our Black children at risk—your child might be reluctant to look for help and challenge the established concept of Black resilience. Or maybe you are the one who's resistant to the idea of professional help for your child because you've been raised to believe that mental distress is a sign of weakness. Be courageous and consider the help of a mental health professional, preferably one with the same cultural background, who will understand some of the stigma associated with depression within Afro-Caribbean spaces.

It may be challenging, but it is possible to raise a creative, confident Black child who knows how to self-advocate and can recognize when he or she is being mistreated. It takes a lot of vigilance and patience. You'll learn as they grow how to best help them succeed in life. You've already taken the biggest step by showing an interest in their future and in their education.

Coping Strategies

If your child is exhibiting signs of acute anxiety or depression, expresses thoughts of suicide, or acts out in dangerous ways, it is imperative that you seek professional help with a licensed therapist right away. In a crisis, you can call the Suicide Prevention Helpline at: 1-800-273 TALK. Make sure you find a therapist who is a good fit for your child, understands his or her needs and is sensitive to the effects of racism. Keep looking until you find the right health care provider for your child. But there are a lot of things you can do to lighten the day-to-day stress of living in a racist society and help lower cortisol levels.

These include:[132]

- Discussing emotional states with your child. Ask them how they are feeling. Validate their feelings and let them know what they are experiencing is normal. Share your own experiences so your child understands that what they are experiencing is common.

---

132   See References: Coping Strategies

- Deep breathing exercises: There are a number of these you can practice, but try breathing in through your nose for a count of four, hold your breath for a count of seven, then exhale through pursed lips for a count of eight.

- Make sure your child is drinking plenty of fluids and eating a well-balanced diet. This will ensure that they are getting the nutrients they need to stay physically healthy.

- Journaling is an excellent way to process emotions and express some of the harder emotions they may not be ready to talk to you about. Respect your child's privacy if they keep a journal. No snooping!

- Exercise! Even just a brisk walk will help lower stress hormones and help stave off depressive episodes.

- Tune out and unplug. Take a break from the news and from social media and focus on the here and now. When kids witness catastrophic or violent events on the news, they sometimes get overwhelmed with feelings of powerlessness. Taking a break from media coverage can help.

- Engage in some hobbies. Whether it's gardening or painting or coloring, hobbies also help with anxiety levels and give kids something they can focus creative energy on.

- Laugh it out. Take time to find fun things to do, like watching a comedy on television, whatever will cause you all to erupt in deep belly laughter. It may seem like it's impossible to laugh at some of the worst moments, but laughing is a great stress relief.

- Spend time with your pets. Pets are excellent for soothing anxiety and creating a calm connection.

- Yoga. Yoga increases flexibility and encourages calm and relaxation.

- Meditation: You can use a guided meditation from one of the many available online, or learn transcendental meditation as a family and practice it.

- Scream it out. Go out into the backyard with a bucket of balls and encourage your kids to let it all out, throw the balls as hard as they can, and scream at the top of their lungs. In a controlled setting, this can release a lot of pent up anger.

- Go out. Sometimes it can help to be out in the world in an environment where things are peaceful and relaxing. Treat your family to a meal at a decent restaurant and just enjoy being out of the house for a night.

- Go to a park and connect with nature. If you live near a beach or a lake, many people find that being near water is soothing.

- Encourage your kids to volunteer. Join them and make it a family effort. While you can work for a cause geared toward racial justice, if your child is having a hard time, they can also do something unrelated, like volunteering at an animal shelter.

- If your family is religious, see if there is a youth group at the church for your child's age group they can join.

- If you find your child is stuck on a bad memory, try grounding exercises to help them focus on the here and now. Make it a game. Using all of the senses identify items in the environment they can interact with. For example, what three things can you hear? What three things do you smell, touch, taste, see? Encourage them to use their senses to actually touch, taste, smell, see, and hear these things.

- If your child is having an anxiety attack, counting exercises sometimes help to disable the panic. Have them count slowly (depending on their age) to a hundred or a thousand. Coupling a counting exercise with walking works even better. Take a walk with them and together count each step. This works by having the left side of the brain take over from the emotional center of the brain. It sometimes takes practice, so be patient.

- Don't be afraid to seek out counseling for your child or as a family. The stigma related to getting help from a licensed professional often prevents Black people from seeking help they need. Don't wait for a crisis to see a counselor, make it a weekly appointment.

If your child learns to self-advocate, they will be better equipped to communicate their needs to you and their teachers, and to let you know when their teachers are falling short or they are experiencing bias at school. They'll be more likely to communicate difficult emotions as well and can help themselves avoid depression and the other physical and mental tolls of racism that put them in danger of developing a chronic medical condition or having suicidal thoughts. You still need to remain vigilant, because even a child who can self-advocate may become overwhelmed and have trouble reaching out for help. Perhaps the best way to ensure your child a bright future is to build them a stable home environment in a safe neighborhood. Next we'll look at ways you can help create a safer home and in your community for your kids.

Chapter 11

How to Help Make Your Community Safer

The importance of a safe community for your child to grow up in cannot be stressed enough. They say, "it takes a village to raise a child," and the environment surrounding your home is that village. It's the place your child will first venture out into as they make their way into the world and explore different experiences and people than they can find at home. Working to ensure your community is safe also helps ease the stress of being the parent of a Black child because you can be reasonably assured that the chances of a racist attack happening are diminished when you have a community watching out for the general welfare of its citizens.

In this chapter, we'll look at some ways to build a stronger, safer community for your child and all the children in your community, and we'll start with your home environment and then look outward at the neighborhood and surrounding area.[133]

At Home

Your home should be an oasis for your child. It should be a safe place they want to anchor themselves and spend time in. Safety is paramount to building a place of security for you and your kids. Start early teaching your children lessons on how to protect themselves from violence and predators. Here are some tips to make your home the preferred destination for your child when they leave the outside world:

- Make sure your home is secure. Install strong locks and impact-safe windows. Have a security system installed. Keep up maintenance on the exterior of the property if you have outside space. Consider installing security cameras outside. Make sure you have a peephole in the main entrance to your home so you can check to see who's outside when someone rings the bell or knocks. Consider getting a dog, not only for companionship, but also to alert you if someone is on your property.

- Starting at an early age, teach your children to be polite and courteous. Make sure "please," "thank you," "yes, sir (or ma'am)," and "no, ma'am (or sir)," are in their vocabularies. Often a hostile reaction can be avoided with the use of common courtesy.

- Stress the importance of remaining drug-free. Studies have shown that drug use is linked to violence, and gun and weapon use. Set a good example for your kids by abstaining from drugs and limiting alcohol consumption to a responsible level.

- Ensure that your children make friends with other kids who are drug- and alcohol-free and avoid violence. Invite their friends into your home and give them a comfortable space in which to congregate. Help them find fun activities to keep them occupied and safe.

- Teach your kids the basics of self-protection. Avoid interactions with strangers. Never go anywhere with someone who isn't on your "safe list" of adults. Make sure they know what to do if you're not home and someone calls or pays a visit. Teach them the safest way to walk to their most-traveled destinations in the neighborhood. Have discussions about personal boundaries with adults and other kids, and let them know they can tell you if someone tries to touch them inappropriately.

- Run through different scenarios with your kids and quiz them on what to do in dangerous situations they may find themselves: What do you do if you find a gun? What do you do if you witness a robbery? What if someone tries to touch your private places? Make sure your kids have a plan of action if one of these situations arises.

- Limit the places your children are allowed to go. Make sure you know their destination and have met the children and parents of people they want to visit or spend the night with.

- If you have a firearm in the home, keep it secure and preferably unloaded with the ammunition stored separately. Keep the safety on and use trigger locks. Teach your children early that guns are dangerous and should not be played with. Always keep your gun safe locked. Everyone, both children and adults, should take a course on gun safety and renew it every year.

The best way to ensure that your children are safe is to teach them to be mindful of their own security and how to maintain it. Encourage them to discover ways to:

- Learn simple, personal safety tips that can help prevent them becoming the victim of a criminal or violent act.

- Learn about "SARA," a rational-based approach to problem solving. The acronym stands for "Scan, analyze, respond, and assess." It's a basic policing strategy, but can be useful if your child runs into a group confrontation with the potential for violence, and is an excellent way to teach them to remain calm in a dangerous situation by remaining objective and searching for solutions to common neighborhood problems.

- Find drug- and alcohol-free events and activities that are happening in your area and ask your children to help find ways they can be made more fun. Encourage your kids to get involved by helping the organizations sponsoring these gatherings, so they'll have practice with event-planning and volunteerism.

Neighborhood Safety Resources for Children

If your child plays outside in your neighborhood, keeping them and the neighborhood safe is an added concern. They'll need to know how to fend for themselves when you're not with them. The following online guides can help you learn to keep your family safe:

1. **Neighborhood Safety Tips for Parents:** This step by step guide can help you keep your kids and neighborhood safe. www.ncpc.org/topics/home-and-neighborhood-safety/ neighborhood-safety

2. **At Home Alone: A Parent's Guide:** If your children are at the age where they can be left alone, you'll want to reference this guide for resources to help them stay safe. www.ncpc.org/ resources/files/pdf/neighborhood-safety/chalone.pdf

3. **The Smart Route to Bicycle Safety:** This guide is put out by the National Crime Prevention Council and helps teach your child bicycle safety and how to avoid having their bicycle stolen. www.ncpc.org/resources/files/pdf/neighborhood-safety/ bikesafety04.pdf

4. **Kidzworld Neighborhood Safety Tips:** Kidzworld designed this guide for children to help them learn tips on how to be safe in their neighborhood and when home alone. www.kidzworld. com/article/8122-neighborhood-safety-tips

5. **Ten New Neighborhood Safety Tips:** From the National Center for Missing and Exploited Children, this guide is for those who are moving to a new neighborhood. The tips here will help you make simple rules to ensure a safe new home. www.parents.com/kids/safety/tips/10-new-neighborhood-safety-tips/

In the Neighborhood

Just a little effort goes a long way in building a safer community. Perhaps the biggest thing you can do is to leave your house and explore the neighborhood. Communities aren't built on their own. It's up to you to take the initiative to build a more united neighborhood. Here are some ideas for things you can do that will increase the level of safety in your community:

1. Get to know your neighbors and their children by name. Introduce yourself and start a conversation with them about the neighborhood.

2. Take part in community-building events by either participating or hosting one. Work with others in the community to reclaim neglected or abandoned spaces. Spread the word about safety initiatives.

3. Explore! Walk around the block. Get out and say hi to the people you meet. You can gauge the safety level best if you spend time observing your neighborhood.

4. Pick up any trash that's thrown on the street near your property. You can also organize a group effort to pick up litter in your community.

5. Help organize regular meetings of the people on your block to discuss how the neighborhood is doing and to check in with each other.

6. Start a neighborhood watch group or another type of community organization. If you see nuisances that aren't necessarily criminal, be sure to report them. Definitely report any crimes to the police as soon as you can.

7. Avoid opportunities that arise for crime. Keep your valuables secured and out of the line of sight.

8. Take and/or organize a self-defense course for people in your community.

9. Work to improve the lighting around your home and in your neighborhood. Learn about safer landscaping techniques and share them with your neighbors.

10. Plan neighborhood tours for the children in your community. Introduce them to friendly neighbors.

11. If you live in an area with a lot of rental properties find out who the landlords are and maintain a list in case you need to report a problem.

12. Take your time driving through your neighborhood. If you live in an area with a lot of children, petition for a traffic study to see if speed bumps or extra stop signs are needed.

13. You can find out more tips on keeping your neighborhood safe at the LAPD's crime prevention website at www.lapdonline. org/crime_prevention/content_basic_view/8807.

Other Resources:

Here are some other resources that can come in handy whether you're just starting to think about the safety of your neighborhood, or you've been a long-time community organizer:

1. **National Neighborhood Watch:** This website can help you search for a neighborhood watch program in your area or register your neighborhood watch group. They also offer training resources and tips on neighborhood safety. www.nnw.org/

2. **Starting a Neighborhood Watch:** A handy step by step guide to setting up a neighborhood watch program in your community. www.ncpc.org/resources/files/pdf/neighborhood-safety/nwstart.pdf

3. **Tools and Resources to Help You Start or Maintain a Neighborhood Watch Program:** From the National Crime Prevention Council, this Neighborhood Watch resource will help you set up a new program in your community or maintain your current Neighborhood Watch Program. www.ncpc.org/topics/home-and-neighborhood-safety/neighborhood-watch

4. **Neighborhood Safety Network:** From the Consumer Product Safety Commission, this resource offers tools to keep you safe in your home and in the area surrounding it. www.cpsc.gov/en/Safety-Education/Neighborhood-Safety-Network/

5. **What Do You Say When…?:** The City of Minneapolis police department offers answers for some of the objections you may get to setting up a neighborhood watch program. www.minneapolismn.gov/www/groups/public/@mpd/documents/webcontent/convert_283649.pdf

6. **How to Use Nextdoor for Crime Prevention:** This article explains how to use the Nextdoor social media app to help prevent crime in your neighborhood by keeping in touch

with your neighbors. help.nextdoor.com/customer/portal/ articles/1019177-how-to-use-nextdoor-for-crime-prevention

7. **Taking Back Your Neighborhood:** This guide from the National Crime Prevention Council explains how you can reclaim your neighborhood by coordinating closely with neighbors and local police. www.ncpc.org/resources/files/pdf/ neighborhood-safety/takeback.pdf

8. **Five Ways to Team Up with Your Neighbors to Keep Crime at Bay:** These tips from SafeWise explain how you and your neighbors can work together to fight criminal activity in your community. www.safewise.com/blog/5-ways-team-neighbors-keep-crime-bay/

Neighborhood Safety Checklists

Checklists and surveys are a quick and easy way to keep organized and ensure that you prevent crime and ensure your neighborhood's safety. Here are a few you may find useful:

1. **Neighborhood Checkup Survey:** Your neighbors can fill out this survey to help you identify safety hazards and security issues in your community. www.ncpc.org/resources/files/pdf/ neighborhood-safety/nghbrchk.ps.pdf

2. **Neighborhood Security Survey:** Use this survey to help you and your neighbors perform a security assessment. www.minneapolismn.gov/www/groups/public/@mpd/documents/webcontent/wcms1p-097403.pdf

3. **Home Security Checklist:** This checklist from the National Crime Prevention Council can help you identify security risks at home and threats to safety in your neighborhood. www.ncpc.org/resources/files/pdf/neighborhood-safety/homechk2.pdf

4. **Checklist for Starting a Neighborhood Watch Program:** This checklist will help you organize and start a neighborhood watch program in your neighborhood. www.ncpc.org/resources/files/pdf/neighborhood-safety/chklist.pdf

In the Community

There's a lot you can do to foster unity within your community, which will not only make your neighborhood safer, it will also make it feel more like home, and may do other unexpected good like raising property values or even just help you find good friends. Here are some suggestions for initiatives you can start:

1. Adopt a road, park or gate entrance.

2. Start a community garden.

3. Design a safer environment for the community.

4. Initiate a community-wide clean-up effort.

5. Meet and support local leaders in the community.

6. Look for youth initiatives or involve local youth in initiatives you start.

7. Organize and/or host an event for your community.

8. Write/publish a community newsletter.

9. Apply for community block grants.

10. Find volunteer opportunities in your neighborhood.

How Technology Can Help

There are some useful social media apps that can help you stay in touch with neighbors and people in elected positions in your community. Here are some suggested ways to connect without leaving your home:

1. Form a Facebook group.

2. Check out Nextdoor.

3. Teach kids (your own and those in the neighborhood) about social media safety.

4. Check out Crimemapping.com for up to date information on criminals and sex offenders in your community.

Use these services to receive updates on criminals and other dangers in your community.

1. **Family Watchdog:** This is a free service that will show you where registered sex offenders and other criminals live. You can sign up for free updates to get alerted when one moves in or out of your community. www.familywatchdog.us/

2. **Neighborhood Scout:** Neighborhood Scout can help provide you key information on crime, sex offenders, and more. www.neighborhoodscout.com/

3. **CrimeReports:** CrimeReports will provide you with information on crimes that have happened in your area. www.crimereports.com/

4. **SpotCrime:** SpotCrime can help you learn about criminal activities such as arson, assaults, burglaries, robberies, theft, and vandalism in your neighborhood. spotcrime.com/

Vote!

One of the best ways of ensuring your neighborhood is a safe one is to make sure you exercise your civic duty and vote for initiatives that promote positive youth programs and discourage youth violence. These help build stronger communities by:

1. Preventing violence in the schools.

2. Responding to the needs of the community.

3. Supporting more peace in the community.

4. Engaging and encouraging kids.

Gentrification and Other Concerns

If you live in a major urban area, chances are you've seen gentrification at work. A poverty-stricken neighborhood suddenly becomes appealing to developers, who buy up the land at low cost, evict the people living there, and rebuild the community so that it's a thriving urban center with high-cost rent and few people of color. There are many reasons why this happens, the most obvious is that Black-owned properties tend to have lower property values, even when they are equal to white-owned properties in terms of location and upkeep. Some studies place the value of Black-owned homes at about 50 percent of the price of white-owned homes.

The result of gentrification is often the displacement of Black families who find themselves priced out of decent neighborhoods and must find another area with concentrated poverty in which to reside. This is disruptive to children and places them at higher risk of behavior problems, lower test scores, and a greater risk of dropping out of school completely.

But why are Black-owned properties so undervalued? There's a combination of factors that lead to this, among them is "redlining" of low-cost/Black neighborhoods by real estate agents, the lack of funding for overall improvement of infrastructure, and implicit bias, which makes buyers perceive homes as less valuable simply because they have Black owners. Realtors are less likely to show Black families as many homes as their white counterparts and often fail to show them homes in desegregated communities. Subprime mortgage brokers tend to concentrate their loans in high Black population centers as well, leading to more foreclosures. It is harder for a Black family, regardless of income or credit to get a low-cost loan, so more Black families tend to have their homes foreclosed on due to predatory lending practices. To be clear, the Fair Housing laws in this country forbid discriminatory lending practices and other discrimination in realtor practices, but they aren't enforced well, and Black people are still subject to rampant implicit bias in both lending and buying practices.

These practices have led to a clear segregation of communities into Black/white or poor vs. upwardly mobile. Put simply, there is less opportunity in Black majority neighborhoods.

Racism in Urban Design

If you travel through poor urban centers anywhere in the United States, you'll see a few things that poor areas have in common. There's a lack of crosswalks, lighting is poor, properties are poorly maintained, and chances are the community is divided by a highway overpass. The reasons for this, according to the Brookings Institute, are intentional.[134] The government and private investors have divested themselves of neighborhoods with a high Black population

---

134   Love (2019)

for decades. Highways were deliberately placed to run through the most impoverished neighborhoods. The lack of infrastructure and safe street crossings leads to other problems like higher gun violence and other crime. The fact that nearly half of all Black children live in impoverished neighborhoods, as compared to white kids of whom only 12 percent live in poverty, sets Black kids up for outright failure, if not simply a pressing set of challenges they must overcome. When communities are segregated, schools are zoned according to community, and more poor Black kids wind up in poorer schools with less resources. It is imperative therefore that in order to build safe streets and stronger communities with more opportunity, we need to address racism in urban design.

Some communities have taken to painting their own crosswalks in an effort to decrease the number of pedestrian fatalities, but that's not really a viable solution. In order to really address the problem, a systemic overhaul is in order. Block grants for urban renewal projects are one method of investing in safer communities, but the main action that needs to be taken is for elected officials to start paying attention to these neglected, overlooked areas and work with local residents to improve the infrastructure.

The Not-So-Hidden Practice of Segregation

A few years ago, some researchers in Illinois invited people to discuss the neighborhoods they lived in and their communities.[135] They placed a simple map of Chicago on the table between them. Inevitably, when discussing their neighborhoods, the discussion turned to race. People pointed to neighborhoods on the outskirts of Chicago and referred to them as white neighborhoods, and pointed out urban centered areas as Black neighborhoods without being

135   Chang (2017)

prompted, even if they hadn't visited the areas themselves. Built into the minds of the study participants, there was a racially segregated idea of the city of Chicago. But why?

Research seems to show there is a good amount of fear in white people that their communities will lose something if they become diversified. It's not just Black families moving into their area that causes "white flight." The same phenomenon occurs when Hispanic or Asian families move into a traditionally white neighborhood, though they are more likely to find a home in a diverse area than Blacks are. A recent PRRI survey showed that half of all Republicans and 1/3 of all Americans believe that racial diversity would have a negative effect on America.

The result of this fear of diversity is that it is often unsafe for Black families to live or for Black individuals to travel through white areas which leads to avoidance and exacerbates the problem of segregation. And for Black families that move into predominantly white areas, there can be consequences as well.

In the 1930s writer Lorraine Hansberry's (A Raisin in the Sun) family took a case to the US Supreme Court when their white neighbors tried to force them out of the neighborhood they had purchased a home in. In the 1950s, Nat King Cole's home was firebombed by his white neighbors. It is still the case that when Black families move to a white suburb, white families move out, or the opposite, that when an area is gentrified, Black families are displaced.

In 1975, a group of Black children in Rosedale, New York unwittingly bicycled into a white supremacist gathering and were pelted with stones and racist slurs. That incident, captured on video and broadcast on Bill Moyers Journal, left a long-lasting impression on the children who were attacked, many of them reported that they still bore painful memories of the incident forty-five years later when they were interviewed by The New York Times. What the children did not know was that Rosedale was in the midst of a shift in demographics as more

> Black families were moving into the area, and white families were vacating in what has been termed "white flight."

According to Danielle Fairbairn-Bland, a psychotherapist who works with children and teenagers in New York City, living in a white neighborhood comes with its own set of concerns about things like self-image:

> For black children growing up in white spaces that don't nurture their identity and don't create a safe space for them to feel confident, it definitely has a direct impact on their self-esteem, their ability to thrive in school, their ability to socialize [...]. It can really skew their view of their role in society because they are usually one of few in a space where they're expected to develop and perform like it's business as usual.[136]

It also may not be any safer for Black children to grow up in predominantly white or equitably mixed neighborhoods. Michael Brown, Trayvon Martin, and John Crawford were all killed in the suburbs. Ahmaud Arbery was in a predominantly white neighborhood. Philando Castile was in an area where the Black population is about 30 percent. And research shows that Black boys feel more anxiety when they are in predominantly white areas.[137]

> **The Negro Motorist Handbook** (a.k.a. The Negro Motorist Green Book, The Negro Traveler's Green Book or simply The Green Book) was an annual guidebook published from 1936 until 1966 by Victor Hugo Green, a New York City mailman. The guide was meant to help middle class Black Americans who had purchased vehicles avoid some of the pitfalls of Jim Crow laws from being refused service to arbitrary arrest. The guide expanded from its focus on New York City

136   Robinson (2020)
137   Chacon (2018)

to include most of the United States, parts of Canada, Mexico, the Caribbean, and Bermuda. Publication ceased after the Civil Rights Act of 1964 made Jim Crow laws obsolete, but there has been a renewed interest in the guide as a historical relic and several of its issues have gone into reprint and have sold well. The New York Public Library has digitized twenty-three of its issues.

White Return: When Gentrification Happens

All over the country, for about the last twenty years or so, diversity has been shifting to white neighborhoods as Asian, Black, and Hispanic families have purchased homes in predominantly white areas. Census figures show that diversification happens this way about 90 percent of the time a community is integrated.[138]

But what often happens as a side effect to diversification is that once their communities are integrated, white families move into neighborhoods where the population is mostly people of color, and quickly price out Black and other minority homeowners, raising rents and driving out Black residents, creating new white communities and displacing Black homeowners and renters in the process. James Baldwin coined the term "Negro Removal" in the 1960s to explain the oftentimes subtle process of gentrification. Its impacts on Black communities are measurable. As the Black population is priced out of its neighborhood, they are forced to relocate to even lower income areas which leads to problems with food choices, as many low-income areas are also food deserts. Some of the other problems Black families face in their new neighborhoods are linked to affordable housing, choice of public or other transportation, quality schools,

---

138   Badger (2019)

exercise facilities or bicycle and walking paths, and established social networks. According to the CDC, there is also an increase in stress, injuries, violence and crime, mental health problems, and a decrease in social and environmental justice.

It also leads to a more frequent occurrence of the criminalization of Black people who remain in the community being gentrified, and an increase in police calls for simply being Black.

Black displacement does not have to occur with gentrification, and sometimes communities do reap the benefits of increased property values without driving out existing residents, but it takes a concerted effort that includes measures such as homestead exemptions that cap property tax rates and ensure Black families can stay in the homes they've lived in for decades.

The best way to avoid gentrification is to work on your community as it stands right now and make improvements to its infrastructure. Apply for some community block or arts grants, lobby your local elected officials. Be vigilant.

Chapter 12

When You're a Non-Black Parent to Your Black Child

We have not yet become a post-racial society, but these days, families look a lot differently than they did even fifty years ago. Non-Black parents are adopting or giving birth to Black and mixed-race children more often, and our understanding of what makes a family has changed as a result. If you are the non-Black parent of a Black or multiracial child, there are some special concerns that you may have about raising your child to be healthy, confident, and happy. It is naïve to think that raising a child who looks different than you isn't complicated by issues of race. Your child will inevitably grow up with a stronger understanding of their identity if you face the issue of race head on, rather than ignoring the physical and social differences they face.

Remember:

- It isn't enough to simply love your child. You'll need to be vigilant and supportive. Your child will need you to put their needs above your own comfort level.

- You'll need to be willing to confront some blatant and/or passive racist views many non-Black people possess, whether consciously or not.

- If you are a non-Black parent raising a mixed-race or Black child, understand that no matter how much you'd like for race not to be an issue, your child is probably going to have to deal with the social ramifications of being Black in a racist society.

Things Your Child Needs

There are special considerations you need to make for your Black child that they won't necessarily know how to communicate to you or even understand that they need. It's your job as their parent to be proactive and make sure their needs are met in these areas.[139]

Expose your children to more people of color. Many children adopted into non-Black families or raised in non-Black neighborhoods report feeling racially isolated. There are places in the United States that are geographically racially segregated. Make sure your child grows up seeing other people of the same racial background regularly. This can mean attending services at a Black church or joining an after-school or weekend program where your child can socialize with people of their race.

Ensure that your Black child has a peer group of children they can play with and socialize with often. Sometimes that means taking a measure as drastic as moving to a new neighborhood. Make sure your children see you socializing with Black friends as well. If you don't have any Black friends, work on finding some.

Be proactive about talking to your child about race. They shouldn't have to wait for you to start having "the Talk" with them. Talking

---

139   See References: When You're a Non-Black Parent to Your Black Child

about race should be an ongoing discussion you have regularly, and you should be prepared to talk about racist incidents when they come up in media coverage; be prepared as well to deal with the emotions that often accompany these events. Understand that this can be difficult. Know that you don't have to pretend to have all the answers. Racism is complicated and not knowing everything is normal. Help your child find answers to their questions. Help them understand that racist ideas are harmful; if they point out that a lady has brown skin, it is not racist, but if they communicate that a Black woman is less attractive than a white woman, be prepared to ask questions and challenge their ideas.

Don't expect that their school will teach them about their history. This means more than trotting out the book on Dr. King each February. It means building them a library of materials at home that they can access whenever they want to read a book or watch a documentary about Black history. This also means you need to be prepared to challenge the administration at your school for either ignoring your child's Blackness or believing that they are a behavior problem. You might have to play an active role in helping your child find Black mentors they can look up to. Ask these mentors questions you may have about raising your child. Pay attention to the interactions your child has with their mentors and take lessons from it.

Keep an open mind. Your child may have a different accent and/ or culture than you. Especially if you are raising a multicultural child, your child may switch accents depending on the social setting. They may adopt customs from one culture over another. They may question, reject or be ashamed of some cultural practices. They may choose not to recognize Christmas in favor of Kwanzaa or some other holiday of their choosing. Be flexible and understanding with them. Remember, your child is trying out identities to see what feels right. Biracial children who are light enough to pass as white may decide not to identify as Black. While you should allow them to freely explore their identities and culture, continue to be diligent in connecting your child with their culture.

If you find yourself deeply disturbed by a biracial child wanting to "pass," preferring to have non-Black friends, and choosing non-Black spaces, if your child seems embarrassed by their Blackness, resist the temptation to "slap the nonsense out of them." Discuss the situation with a counselor to decide whether you should accept this denial of heritage (maybe you don't want your child to worry about race), or instead nip it in the bud. Should you say, "Let's talk about who you really are and why you're eclipsing part of yourself"? "We're not in the Jim Crow era anymore, you don't have to pass"? Should you push your child to face possible peer pressure head on and shed what could be internalized racism? Discuss these important questions with a professional as there may be a serious emotional issue to address. It could be that your child is being bullied for their Blackness. It could be that the Black people in their lives are not effectively modeling Blackness. Find out! Being part of a strong network of parents of Black children can be a life-saver; it will allow you to have important conversations, as no book can cover *all* the issues you will face while raising a Black kid.

In this excerpt of Brian Crooks's story from Facebook, he writes about the lack of Black representation during his formative years through adulthood:

I've never had a Black boss. I played football from middle school through senior year of high school and only had one Black coach in that whole time. Not just head coaches, I'm talking about assistants and position coaches. I've had two Black teachers in my entire life. One was for my Harlem Renaissance class, and one was for my sign language class. I've never been to a Black doctor, or a Black dentist. I've never been pulled over by a Black police officer. What I'm trying to explain is that, in thirty-one years, I've seen three Black people in a position of authority. Think about what that does to the psyche of a growing young man. I remember being excited just a few years ago when we started to see Black people in commercials without there being gospel or hip-hop music in the background (remember that McDonald's commercial where the little kid was pop-locking with the chicken McNuggets?).

Some Other Considerations

Raising a Black or multiracial child if you are not a person of color can be complicated. In addition to managing the dynamic within your own home, you may find yourself dealing with relatives and others who question your motives or are outright racist about your decision. Here are some things to keep in mind.

It might be uncomfortable. Talk about race with the people around you. Talk about it often, and be proud of your child. White fragility is not your friend; it never was. You're strong enough to handle relatives and naysayers. Your child's Blackness should not be the unspoken thing in the room that everyone is afraid to talk about. Invite your relatives to have an open discussion with you about race. You're going to have to get used to being vigilant. Sticking up for your child doesn't just mean calling out overt racists or speaking up for your child when they get harassed by a cop. It means watching out for their best interests *all the time* and being prepared for microaggressions from unlikely sources.

For a productive discussion on race with people in your family or friend circle who may hold biases, watch Verna Myers' TED Talk "How to Overcome Our Biases, Walk Boldly Toward Them." www.youtube.com/watch?v=uYyvbgINZkQ.

Be conscious of the power dynamic in your family. As a non-Black parent, it is easy to slip into white supremacy within your own family dynamic. Learning about racism is already an ugly process, be prepared to loosen up some of the structure in your own family and cut off any family members who aren't willing and/or able to do the work to confront their own racist ideas and attitudes. Make sure that your child's friendships with non-Black children are not modeled on white supremacy, where your child feels honored to be worthy to have a non-Black kid for a friend. Listen for any statements that link race with a value judgment, and be prepared to step in if you hear them to correct the statement. (For example, "Barbie is more beautiful than Doc McStuffins because she's white and has blond hair.")

You'll probably feel some pressure about how to bring up your children from relatives outside your nuclear family. Do what you feel is best always.

Emphasize the beauty of Blackness. This means accepting and understanding that there are some physical differences between you and your child. It also means a lot more than buying your child toys that look like him/her. It means encouraging your child to accept their unique beauty, and the beauty of being Black. Watch what you say: Pay attention to your own biases and any stereotypes you may rely on. Again, your kids are listening to and learning from you.

Check yourself! How much diversity is in your own daily life? If you don't have many/any Black friends, it may be time for you to reach out and cultivate some meaningful relationships with Black families. Find ways to not only introduce diversity into your daily life, but also make connections with potential allies. If your child is one of only two Black children in their class, for example, approach the other child's parents and introduce yourself.

Go beyond diversity. Become an anti-racist activist. Take part in the protest movement in whatever way feels most comfortable to you, even if it's reaching out to elected officials and demanding change.

The Backlash of Raising a Multiracial Family

If you are already raising a black or mixed-race child, you are (unfortunately) probably already aware of the backlash that comes with adopting or fostering a child outside of your race. People can be blatantly rude and judgmental about mixed-race families, and often don't watch what they say. If you are still considering a mixed-race or Black adoption, be prepared. You will likely hear some extremely hurtful and racist things that might shock you. White parents tend to hear criticism that they won't be able to properly groom a Black child or worse, that they are a "white savior" and should be commended for rescuing a Black child from a life of addiction and crime. Both statements are just ignorant, and you should call anyone who says such nonsense out as soon as you hear it. Not everyone will understand your reasons for wanting to raise a child who looks differently than you.

Be aware, there is a double standard that exists between white and Black adoptive and foster parents who raise a child outside of their race. Admittedly, fewer Black families raise white children, but it does happen. Black foster parents and Black adoptive parents of white children also face backlash when they adopt or foster outside of their race. Most often, they are told that they should have left a white child to be raised by "their own kind" and that they are robbing the child of the privilege of growing up in a white home. Some Black parents of white children have reported that they are followed or photographed and suspected of kidnapping their white child.

You may hear some things from other kids (maybe your own kids, if you also have non-Black kids in the home) about your Black child that you should call out immediately:

1. **"Why does her hair look like that? It's weird."** Respond with: "It's not weird. People have all different kinds of textures to their hair, and it is all beautiful in different ways."

2. **"That kid is dirty!"** Respond with: "No, he's not dirty. He has more melanin in his skin. We all have melanin, but some of us have more than others. People come in many different colors."

3. **"We didn't play with them because they are not cool"** (code for "Black" or "brown"). Don't be complacent. Address it right away. "How would you feel if someone wouldn't play with you because of your race or skin color?" Please note that older children might not even acknowledge the exclusion they submitted their peers to. Be on the lookout for reprehensible attitudes and behaviors.

4. **"That Black doll isn't as pretty as this white doll."** Respond with: "I don't agree. I think that Black doll is very pretty. Look, she has beautiful brown skin and hair."

5. **"I'm color-blind."** Respond with: "It's okay to notice differences in how people look from one another—those differences are real. The problem is when we make the mistake of thinking that a certain color means one is better than the other."

6. **"Black kids like to play with their own kind."** Respond with: "How do you feel thinking that? Do you really believe that is true? Why don't you try to make friends with people who look a little differently than all your other friends? You might be surprised to learn you have a lot in common."

Do Transracial Adoption and Multiracial Families Harm Black Culture?

In 1972, the National Association of Black Social Workers called transracial adoption "cultural genocide." Whether they were correct in making this claim is still a topic for debate. Some people claim that the best way to fight racism is to adopt children of different races, and to build multiracial families, because there is no surer way of fighting bias than by loving a child of a different race. Others say that no non-Black (or multiracial) family can ever support the kind of cultural upbringing a Black child needs to feel comfortable with their own race.

It is certainly possible to harm individual children by ignoring their need to be exposed to Black culture and Black role models, but this can be mitigated by being mindful of your child's needs and doing everything you can to ensure they have a comprehensive understanding of what it means to be Black in a non-Black or multiracial family.

You're reading this book, aren't you? You're doing the right thing!

Love isn't everything your child needs, but don't underestimate the power of love. If you expose your children early to people who look like them and have a culture in common with them, and if you continue to help them bridge racial divides, you're off to a good start.

A non-Black parent to a Black kid recently shared her experience with me:

> When we adopted Jordan many years ago, I was terrified: I lacked any understanding of what it meant to be a Black child, let alone what it'd take to raise one. My husband and I extrapolated, and exposed him to other Black people, and kept open communication about the practical realities of the different cultures, but we still worried

about failing him. We did our best: he had Black mentors, he had Black friends, and we encouraged all sorts of activities that promote Black culture. Yet, we felt clueless. We came later to realize that this feeling of powerlessness, this deep-seated fear, simply comes with the territory. In the end, we raised a beautiful boy who feels confident in his Black skin.

Raising a Black or mixed-race child is as joyful and rewarding as raising any other child. There will be added challenges, but you can raise a happy, healthy, well-adjusted kid who understands their cultural heritage and is an adamant anti-racist. Start with love, and remain vigilant. Find them role models, and be ready to make some tough parenting decisions. And remember, parenting isn't meant to be easy. It can be the most difficult task in the world, no matter how well-behaved and brilliant the child may be.

Conclusion & Acknowledgments

Raising a confident, empowered Black child will be one of the most fulfilling experiences you'll have in your life. It won't be easy, but picking up this book and reading it is a good sign that you are invested in seeing your child develop into a healthy, happy adult. As you watch your child grow and you do your best to nurture them along their path, you'll face many positive milestones. If you remain committed to your child's success, they have a good chance of having a happy, fulfilling life.

As I worked on this book, Black Lives Matter protests in Portland, Oregon, and other major cities across the United States continued to dominate the news, so I was constantly mindful of the stakes for Black children in America, but also hopeful that the calls for equal justice would finally bring some real, lasting reform. There are no easy answers for many of the questions I know parents of Black kids need answers to, and the most challenging of these questions is "why?" Why is it like this in the world today? Why haven't we fixed these issues already?

The system of racism makes no logical sense. If any segment of society is oppressed, even to the advantage of another group, the whole society is weaker as a result of the oppression. But it's a system we've all inherited, and the structure is one that will take many hands, and probably many years, to dismantle. Perhaps the boldest step you can take and the greatest contribution you can make toward tearing it down is to raise a child who knows their worth and is strong enough to continue the work of building something better for the future. The best bit of advice I can give you is to love your Black child and foster their individuality. In a world that classifies people by color, nurturing a strong Black child so that they develop a solid sense of identity is a courageous, bold, and revolutionary act. If I can leave you with any last words, they are the same ones I'd urge you to tell your child frequently: You can do this. I believe in you.

I'd like to take a moment to thank everyone who helped me with the considerable research and editing that went into writing this book: Jan Becker, you've been a true ally; thanks for directing me toward many of the resources I needed. Un grand merci to writer and social justice warrior Fabienne Josaphat, a woman who exemplifies strong motherhood, and whose sharp knowledge of Black history was inspiring. Mèsi anpil to my sister Patricia Fièvre who's quite the awesome developmental editor (and little bit of a life coach too!). To Katherine Rosario: muchas gracias. A caring and gifted child therapist, Katherine brings order to many families (and to this book, too!). To my friend and colleague Lisa McGuinness, who was very generous in reviewing a chapter from this book, and to Brian Crooks, whose Facebook testimony gave me chills.

To my husband, Thomas, the ultimate ally in a world eager to discard me.

To my mother, Carmita, and my grandmothers, Simone and Clara. I hope you're proud of me.

To my aunt Marlene who was the first adult to really *see* me. You took my writing seriously when I was just a tween—and now look at the beast you created!

To my sisters Nathalie and Jenny who (just like Patricia) allowed me to experience motherhood vicariously. (Bisous, bisous, Naïké, Clélie, Marc-Olivier, Nicolas, and Imane!)

To Anthony, my brother from another mother—who recently became a father for the second time.

To my editors at Mango Publishing who trusted me with the herculean task of writing this book. Chris and Brenda, thank you for your mentorship. Robin, thanks for accommodating some of those crazy deadlines, and Daniel, know that I appreciate you very much.

A special thank you to Roberto, Mango designer extraordinaire. Everything you do is beautiful.

I dedicate this book to all my Black students whom I've been honored to serve for over fifteen years.

References

Introduction

- Cooper-Jones, Wanda. "How Was My Son Ahmaud Arbery's Murder Not a Hate Crime?" *The New York Times*. June 9, 2020. Accessed September 19, 2020. www.nytimes.com/2020/06/09/opinion/hate-crime-bill-ahmaud-arbery.html.

- Costello, Darcy and Tessa Duval. "Who was Breonna Taylor? What we know about the Louisville ER tech fatally shot by police." *Courier Journal*. May 12, 2020. Accessed September 19, 2020. www.courier-journal.com/story/news/local/2020/05/12/breonna-taylor-case-what-know-louisville-emt-killed-cops/3110066001.

- Fernandez, Manny and Audra D.S. Burch. "George Floyd, from 'I Want to Touch the World' to 'I Can't Breathe.'" *The New York Times*. July 29, 2020. Accessed September 19, 2020. www.nytimes.com/article/george-floyd-who-is.html.

- McDonald, Autumn. "Black Parents Know 'the Talk' Too Well. It's White Parents' Turn." *Slate Magazine*. June 15, 2020. Accessed September 19, 2020. slate.com/human-interest/2020/06/white-parents-the-talk-racism-police-brutality.html.

- Welch, Cameron "Young Black Man Shares His Mother's Unwritten Rules." Good Morning America Digital. YouTube. June 3, 2020. Accessed September 24, 2020. www.youtube.com/watch?v=VuZ6vcCF74g.

Chapter 1: The Talk: An Avoidable Conversation

- Anderson, Melinda D. "Why Are So Many Preschoolers Getting Suspended?" *The Atlantic*. December 7, 2015. Accessed September 24, 2020. www.theatlantic.com/education/archive/2015/12/why-are-so-many-preschoolers-getting-suspended/418932/.

- Grose, Jessica. "Talking to Kids About Racism, Early and Often." *The New York Times*. June 3, 2020. Accessed September 19, 2020. www.nytimes.com/2020/06/03/parenting/kids-books-racism.html.

- Holohan, Meghan. "How to talk to kids about racism, protests and injustice." Today.com. June 1, 2020. Accessed September 19, 2020. www.today.com/parents/how-talk-kids-about-racism-protests-injustice-t182929.

- Kelly, David J. et al. "Three-month-olds, but not newborns, prefer own-race faces." *Developmental Science*. November 8, 2005. Accessed September 19, 2020. www.ncbi.nlm.nih.gov/pmc/articles/PMC2566511.

- Lopez, German. "Black Parents Describe 'The Talk' They Give to Their Children about Police." Vox. August 8, 2016. Accessed September 19, 2020. www.vox.com/2016/8/8/12401792/police-black-parents-the-talk.

- Paschall-Brown, Gail. "Teen's video highlights talk many black parents have with children about racism, law enforcement." Channel 2. June 5, 2020. Accessed September 19, 2020. www.wesh.com/article/teens-video-highlights-talk-many-black-parents-have-with-children-about-racism-law-enforcement/32786088#.

- Timmis, Gabbi. "How to Talk to Kids about Race and Racism." Today.com. June 1, 2019. Accessed September 19, 2020. www.

today.com/parenting-guides/how-talk-kids-about-race-racism-t179138.

- Widra, Emily. "Stark racial disparities in murder victimization persist, even as overall murder rate declines." Prison Policy Initiative. May 3, 2018. Accessed September 19, 2020. www.prisonpolicy.org/blog/2018/05/03/homicide_overtime/.

- Ziyad, Hari. "How the Myth That All Black Parents Give Kids 'the Talk' about Police Is Used to Silence Resistance." The Black Youth Project. October 29, 2019. Accessed September 19, 2020. blackyouthproject.com/how-the-myth-that-all-black-parents-give-kids-the-talk-about-police-is-used-to-silence-resistance/.

Chapter 2: How to Talk to Your Baby or Toddler About Race

- "11 Learning Activities to Help Discuss Race with Kids." Chicago Parent. July 14, 2020. Accessed September 19, 2020. www.chicagoparent.com/learn/education-workshops/activities-to-discuss-race-with-kids/.

- "An age-by-age guide to talking to your kids about racism." Motherly. n.d. Accessed September 19, 2020. www.mother.ly/child/talking-to-kids-about-racism-age-by-age.

- Edwards-Luce, Aubrey. "Racism Is Hurting Black Children in Schools, Hospitals—Even Day Care—and It's up to Adults to Protect Them." MarketWatch. June 29, 2020. Accessed September 20, 2020. www.marketwatch.com/story/racism-is-hurting-black-children-in-schools-day-care-even-hospitals-and-its-up-to-adults-to-protect-them-2020-06-29.

- Lakhani, Nina. "America Has an Infant Mortality Crisis. Meet the Black Doulas Trying to Change That." The Guardian. November 25, 2019. Accessed September 19, 2020. www.

theguardian.com/us-news/2019/nov/25/african-american-doula-collective-mothers-toxic-stress-racism-cleveland-infant-mortality-childbirth.

- Salam, Maya. "For Serena Williams, Childbirth Was a Harrowing Ordeal. She's Not Alone." *The New York Times.* January 11, 2018. Accessed September 19, 2020. www.nytimes.com/2018/01/11/sports/tennis/serena-williams-baby-vogue.html.

Chapter 3: How to Talk to Young Children About Race

- Anderson, Melinda D. "Why Are So Many Preschoolers Getting Suspended?" *The Atlantic.* December 7, 2015. Accessed September 24, 2020. www.theatlantic.com/education/archive/2015/12/why-are-so-many-preschoolers-getting-suspended/418932/.

- Arnold-Ratliff, Katie. "Anti-Racism for Kids: An Age-by-Age Guide to Fighting Hate." Parents.com. June 2, 2020. Accessed September 19, 2020. www.parents.com/parenting/better-parenting/advice/how-to-teach-your-kids-to-fight-hate-an-age-by-age-guide/.

- Asmelash, Leah. "Student Can't Walk at Graduation Unless He Cuts His Dreadlocks." CNN. January 24, 2020. Accessed September 19, 2020. www.cnn.com/2020/01/23/us/barbers-hill-isd-dreadlocks-deandre-arnold-trnd/index.html.

- Associated Press. "2 Middle School Girls Charged with Racist Attack on Bus." US News & World Report. September 25, 2019. Accessed September 19, 2020. www.usnews.com/news/best-states/new-york/articles/2019-09-25/2-middle-school-girls-charged-with-racist-attack-on-bus.

- Bonvillian, Crystal. "School's Failure to Stop Racist, Sexist Bullying Led to 9-Year-Old Girl's Suicide, Lawsuit States." WFXT. January 17, 2020. Accessed September 19, 2020. www. boston25news.com/news/trending/schools-failure-stop-racist-sexist-bullying-led-9-year-old-girls-suicide-lawsuit-states/ X7EZ7YL6TVGG3H2WBCF3HEL2PE/.

- Bulman, May. "Children as Young as Seven 'Victims of Racist Abuse' on Football Pitch." *The Independent*. May 6, 2019. Accessed September 19, 2020. www.independent.co.uk/ news/uk/home-news/football-racism-discrimination-young-children-seven-bame-a8901251.html.

- Chappell, Bill. "Racist Assault at a Child's Birthday Party Yields Long Prison Terms in Georgia." Npr.org. February 28, 2017. Accessed September 20, 2020. www.npr.org/sections/ thetwo-way/2017/02/28/517688757/racist-assault-on-a-childs-birthday-party-yields-long-prison-terms-in-georgia.

- Cotnam, Hallie. "Cornwall Girl Victim of Racist Attack on School Bus, Mother Says." CBC. June 22, 2020. Accessed September 19, 2020. www.cbc.ca/news/canada/ottawa/ racist-attack-cornwall-school-bus-daughter-taunted-mother-demands-change-1.5615346.

- Feris, Sachi. "5 Tips for Talking About Race with Children." Facing Today. June 23, 2015. Accessed September 19, 2020. facingtoday.facinghistory.org/5-tips-for-talking-about-race-with-children.

- Herbert, Ian. "Teenagers Jailed for Racist Attack on Asian Children." *The Independent*. August 17, 2005. Accessed September 19, 2020. www.independent.co.uk/news/ uk/crime/teenagers-jailed-for-racist-attack-on-asian-children-306422.html.

- McCarthy, Claire. "How Racism Harms Children" Harvard Health Blog. September 14, 2019. Accessed September 1,

2020. www.health.harvard.edu/blog/how-racism-harms-children-2019091417788.

- Picheta, Rob. "Children 'whitening Skin to Avoid Racism' as Hate Crimes against Minors Rise." CNN. May 30, 2019. Accessed September 19, 2020. www.cnn.com/2019/05/30/uk/britain-children-racism-hate-crime-gbr-intl/index.html.

- "SC Attorney Says Black 11 Year Old Was Victim of Racist Attack." ABC Columbia. May 20, 2020. Accessed September 19, 2020. www.abccolumbia.com/2020/05/19/sc-attorney-says-black-11-year-old-was-victim-of-racist-attack/.

- "The Impact of Racism on Children's Health." Dayton Children's. June 4, 2020. Accessed September 19, 2020. www.childrensdayton.org/the-hub/impact-racism-childrens-health.

- "Thinking about Social Justice through Crafts and Conversation." Anti-Defamation League. n.d. Accessed September 20, 2020. www.adl.org/education/resources/tools-and-strategies/thinking-about-social-justice-through-crafts-and.

- "Three-year-old child injured in 'racist' assault in Dresden." Thelocal.de. 11 June 2020. Accessed September 19, 2020. www.thelocal.de/20200611/three-year-old-child-injured-in-racist-assault-in-dresden.

Chapter 4: How to Talk to Your Teens and Tweens About Race

- Dastagir, Alia E. "George Floyd. Ahmaud Arbery. Breonna Taylor. What do we tell our children?" *USA Today*. May 31, 2020. Accessed September 19, 2020. www.usatoday.com/story/news/nation/2020/05/31/how-talk-kids-racism-racial-violence-police-brutality/5288065002/.

- Leavenworth, Jesse. "White Man Charged in Manchester Racist Attack Used Slur against a Black Police Officer during Prior Arrest, Warrant Says." Courant.com. June 23, 2020. Accessed September 20, 2020. www.courant.com/breaking-news/hc-br-manchester-race-charges-warrant-20200623-5dtqbp7x6faszbyf7qv2kp33v4-story.html.

- McDermott, Marie Tae. "Talking to Kids About Racism." *The New York Times*. June 5, 2020. Accessed September 19, 2020. www.nytimes.com/2020/06/05/us/talking-to-kids-about-racism.html.

Chapter 5: Engage in Activism

- Bethea, Alana. "Marsai Martin Is Just One of 15 Young Black Entrepreneurs Making Bank." BET. August 16, 2019. Accessed September 19, 2020. www.bet.com/style/living/2019/08/16/15-under-15-kid-bosses.html.

- Bregel, Sarah. "7 Important Tips for Staying Safe When Taking Kids to Black Lives Matter Demonstrations." LittleThings.com. June 2, 2020. Accessed September 19, 2020. www.littlethings.com/black-lives-matter-protesting-safely-kids/2.

- Burton, Nylah. "Meet the young activists of color who are leading the charge against climate disaster." Vox. October 11, 2019. Accessed September 19, 2020. www.vox.com/identities/2019/10/11/20904791/young-climate-activists-of-color.

- Fitzpatrick, Felicia. "12 Ways You Can Be an Activist Without Going to a Protest." Shine. August 17, 2017. Accessed September 19, 2020. advice.shinetext.com/articles/12-ways-you-can-be-an-activist-without-going-to-a-protest/.

- Kim, Jin David. "Teens from Across Southeast PA Speak Out Against Racism in PCCY's Teen Town Hall." PPCY. June 12,

2020. Accessed September 19, 2020. www.pccy.org/news/pccy-pr-teens-talk-racism-town-hall-quotes-video/.

- Mosley, Tonya. "Merriam-Webster To Revise the Definition of Racism After Receiving Recent Graduate's Letter." wbur. June 12, 2020. Accessed September 19, 2020. www.wbur.org/hereandnow/2020/06/12/merriam-webster-racism-definition.

- Nardino, Meredith. "10 Young Racial Justice Activists You Should Know." Do Something. Fall 2019. Accessed September 19. 2020. www.dosomething.org/us/articles/10-racial-justice-activists-you-should-know.

- Steiger, Kay. "10 of America's Most Daring Young Black Activists." *The Nation.* March 3, 2011. Accessed September 19, 2020. www.thenation.com/article/archive/10-americas-most-daring-young-black-activists/.

- Wicker, Jewel. "5 Young Black Activists Making History Right Now." *Teen Vogue.* February 28, 2019. Accessed September 19, 2020. www.teenvogue.com/story/5-young-black-activists-making-history-right-now.

- Xue, Hannah. "#BlackLivesMatter: The young Black activists using social media to lead the fight for equality." Assembly. June 15, 2020. Accessed September 19, 2020. assembly.malala.org/stories/young-black-activists-to-follow-on-social.

Allyship

- "Checklist for While Allies Against Racism." Power Shift. n.d. Accessed September 19, 2020. www.powershift.org/sites/default/files/resources/files/checklist-for-white-allies.pdf.

- Kivel, Paul. "Guidelines for Being Strong White Allies." Racial Equity Tools. 2006. Accessed September 19, 2020. www.racialequitytools.org/resourcefiles/kivel3.pdf.

- Pruitt, Kenneth. "Atticus Finch and Our Mythological Whiteness." Diversity Awareness Partnership. July 17, 2015. Accessed September 19, 2020. dapinclusive.org/news/atticus-finch-and-our-mythological-whiteness/.

Chapter 6: Racial Profiling

- Weir, Kirsten. "Policing in Black & White." American Psychological Association. 2016. Accessed September 19, 2020. www.apa.org/monitor/2016/12/cover-policing.

- Yan, Holly. "This Is Why Everyday Racial Profiling Is So Dangerous." CNN. 2018. Accessed September 19, 2020. www.cnn.com/2018/05/11/us/everyday-racial-profiling-consequences-trnd/index.html.

Police Encounters

- CNN Library. "Controversial Police Encounters Fast Facts." CNN. April 5, 2015. Accessed September 19, 2020. www.cnn.com/2015/04/05/us/controversial-police-encounters-fast-facts/index.html.

- "Know Your Rights: Stopped by Police." American Civil Liberties Union. 2019. Accessed September 19, 2020. www.aclu.org/know-your-rights/stopped-by-police/.

- "What You Need to Know about Police Encounters." Fighter Law. n.d. Accessed September 19, 2020. www.fighterlaw.com/criminal-law-101/crime-defenses/police-encounters/.

When People Downplay the Problem

- Clayton, Aubrey. "The Statistical Paradox of Police Killings." Boston Globe. June 11, 2020. Accessed September 19, 2020.

www.bostonglobe.com/2020/06/11/opinion/statistical-
paradox-police-killings.

- Coates, Ta-Nehisi. "Black People Are Not Ignoring 'Black
  on Black' Crime." *The Atlantic.* August 15, 2014. Accessed
  September 19, 2020. www.theatlantic.com/national/
  archive/2014/08/black-people-are-not-ignoring-black-on-
  black-crime/378629/.

- Massie, Victoria M. "Why Asking Black People about
  'Black-on-Black Crime' Misses the Point." Vox. April
  28, 2016. Accessed September 19, 2020. www.vox.
  com/2016/4/28/11510274/black-on-black-crime-poverty.

- Ross, Cody T. "A Multi-Level Bayesian Analysis of Racial Bias
  in Police Shootings at the County-Level in the United States,
  2011–2014." Edited by Peter James Hills. *PLOS One.* November
  5, 2015. Accessed September 19, 2020. doi.org/10.1371/journal.
  pone.0141854.

- Smith, Troy L. "Stop Using 'Black-on-Black' Crime to
  Deflect Away from Police Brutality." Cleveland.com. June
  14, 2020. Accessed September 19, 2020. www.cleveland.com/
  news/2020/06/stop-using-black-on-black-crime-to-deflect-
  away-from-police-brutality.html

- "The Biggest Lie in the White Supremacist Propaganda
  Playbook: Unraveling the Truth About 'Black-on-White
  Crime." Southern Poverty Law Center. 2018. Accessed
  September 19, 2020. www.splcenter.org/20180614/biggest-lie-
  white-supremacist-propaganda-playbook-unraveling-truth-
  about-%E2%80%98black-white-crime.

Interesting Facts

- Abrams, Abigail. "Black and Disabled People at Risk in Police
  Encounters." *Time.* June 25, 2020. Accessed September 19,
  2020. time.com/5857438/police-violence-black-disabled/.

- Desilver, Drew et al. "10 Things We Know about Race and Policing in the US" Pew Research Center. June 3, 2020. Accessed September 19, 2020. www.pewresearch.org/fact-tank/2020/06/03/10-things-we-know-about-race-and-policing-in-the-u-s/.

How to Be Safe during a Police Encounter

- "5 Key Safety Tips for Police Encounters." The Nieves Law Firm. May 20, 2017. Accessed September 19, 2020. thenieveslawfirm.com/blog/5-key-safety-tips-for-police-encounters/.

- "10 Ways to Make Your Police Encounter Safer (Especially for Minorities)." DDD Dallas Bail Bonds. June 7, 2019. Accessed September 19, 2020. dallascountybailbondstx.com/10-ways-to-make-your-police-encounter-safer-especially-for-minorities/.

- "A Lawyer's Advice for Black Men at Traffic Stops: 'Comply Now, Contest Later.' " NPR.org. August 1, 2015. Accessed September 19, 2020. www.npr.org/2015/08/01/428420359/a-lawyers-advice-for-black-men-at-traffic-stops-comply-now-contest-later.

- Ali, Maz. "Ways to Help Fight Anti-Black Police Violence." Earthjustice. June 5, 2020. Accessed September 19, 2020. earthjustice.org/blog/2020-june/ways-to-help-fight-anti-black-police-violence.

- "Get Home Safely: 10 Rules of Survival." PBS. 2019. Accessed September 19, 2020. www.pbs.org/black-culture/connect/talk-back/10_rules_of_survival_if_stopped_by_police/.

- Hajebian, Haleh. "10 Ways to Have a Safe Police Encounter." Houston Bail Bonds. June 11, 2019. Accessed September 19, 2020. abc-bailbonds.com/10-ways-to-have-a-safe-police-encounter/.

- "Having 'The Talk': How Families Prepare Black Children for Police Interactions." WTTW News. June 8, 2020. Accessed September 19, 2020. news.wttw.com/2020/06/08/having-talk-how-families-prepare-black-children-police-interactions.

- Nettles, Arionne and Monica Eng. "Having 'The Talk': Expert Guidance on Preparing Kids for Police Interactions." Npr. org. August 27, 2019. Accessed September 19, 2020. www.npr.org/local/309/2019/08/27/754459083/having-the-talk-expert-guidance-on-preparing-kids-for-police-interactions.

- Plourde, Arienne, and Amelia Thompson. "The Talk: Surviving Police Encounters While Black." Utne. 2017. Accessed September 19, 2020. www.utne.com/community/police-racial-discrimination-zm0z17uzcwil.

Living while Black

- Goodnough, Abby. "Harvard Professor Jailed; Officer Is Accused of Bias." *The New York Times.* July 20, 2009. Accessed September 19, 2020. www.nytimes.com/2009/07/21/us/21gates.html.

- Griggs, Brandon. "Here Are All the Mundane Activities for Which Police Were Called on African-Americans This Year." CNN. 2018. Accessed September 19, 2020. www.cnn.com/2018/12/20/us/living-while-black-police-calls-trnd/index.html.

- Lockhart, P.R. "Race, Police, and the Dangers of #LivingWhileBlack." Vox. August 2018. Accessed September 19, 2020. www.vox.com/explainers/2018/8/1/17616528/racial-profiling-police-911-living-while-black.

The Talk, by Age

- Young, Saundra. "Deaths Shape How Black Parents Navigate 'The Talk.' " WebMD. June 8, 2020. Accessed September 19, 2020. www.webmd.com/mental-health/news/20200608/deaths-shape-how-black-parents-navigate-the-talk.

Time to Shift Focus

- Belk, Judy. "Opinion: As a Black Parent, I Need to Update 'the Talk' I Have with My Kids about Police." *Los Angeles Times*. November 3, 2019. Accessed September 19, 2020. www.latimes.com/opinion/story/2019-11-03/african-americans-police-talk-kids-botham-jean-atatiana-jefferson.

- Blake, John. "Black Parents Wonder If 'The Talk' Is Still Effective in Keeping Their Children Safe." MSN.com. May 29, 2020. Accessed September 20, 2020. www.msn.com/en-us/news/us/black-parents-wonder-if-the-talk-is-still-effective-in-keeping-their-children-safe/ar-BB14LFV2.

- Blake, John. "George Floyd. Ahmaud Arbery. Breonna Taylor. What Can Black Parents Possibly Tell Their Kids Now about Staying Safe?" CNN. May 29, 2020. Accessed September 20, 2020. www.cnn.com/2020/05/29/us/black-parents-children-safety-talk-blake/index.html.

- Hart, Benji. "Giving Black Children 'The Talk' Won't Save Them from Police Brutality." HuffPost. May 3, 2017. Accessed September 19, 2020. www.huffpost.com/entry/its-time-to-rethink-the-talk-teaching-black-kids_b_590a133ee4b084f59b49fef0.

Chapter 7: Systemic Racism: Explainer

- "8 Everyday Ways to Fight Racism." NNEDV. March 21, 2017. Accessed September 19, 2020. nnedv.org/latest_update/8-everyday-ways-to-fight-racism/.

- "Bearing the Burden: How Racism-Related Stress Hurts America's Black Mothers and Babies." Community commons. n.d. Accessed September 20, 2020. www.communitycommons. org/entities/25e83f07-6cb2-40ab-9e8c-2d4613af8d19.

- Blow, Charles M. "Call a Thing a Thing." *The New York Times.* July 8, 2020. Accessed September 24, 2020. www.nytimes. com/2020/07/08/opinion/racism-united-states.html.

- Carson, Ann E. "Prisoners in 2014." US Department of Justice. 2015. Accessed September 19, 2020. www.bjs.gov/content/pub/ pdf/p14.pdf.

- Collins, Sean. "The Systemic Racism Black Americans Face, Explained in 9 Charts." Vox. June 17, 2020. Accessed September 19, 2020. www.vox.com/2020/6/17/21284527/ systemic-racism-black-americans-9-charts-explained.

- "How to end institutional racism." Contexts. April 7, 2016. Accessed September 19, 2020. contexts.org/blog/how-to-end-institutional-racism/.

- Kerby, Sophia. "The Top 10 Most Startling Facts About People of Color and Criminal Justice in the United States." Center for American Progress. March 13, 2012. Accessed September 19, 2020. www.americanprogress.org/issues/race/ news/2012/03/13/11351/the-top-10-most-startling-facts-about-people-of-color-and-criminal-justice-in-the-united-states/.

- Nesbit, Jeff. "Institutional Racism Is Our Way of Life." *US News & World Report.* May 6, 2015. Accessed September 19, 2020. www.usnews.com/news/blogs/at-the-edge/2015/05/06/ institutional-racism-is-our-way-of-life.

- O'Dowd, Mary Frances. "Explainer: What Is Systemic Racism and Institutional Racism?" The Conversation. February 5, 2020. Accessed September 19, 2020. theconversation. com/explainer-what-is-systemic-racism-and-institutional-racism-131152.

- "On Views of Race and Inequality, Blacks and Whites Are Worlds Apart." Pew Research Center's Social & Demographic Trends Project. June 27, 2016. Accessed September 19, 2020. www.pewsocialtrends.org/2016/06/27/on-views-of-race-and-inequality-blacks-and-whites-are-worlds-apart/.

- Perry, Andre M. "Discriminatory Housing Practices Are Leading to the Devaluation of Black Americans." Brookings. February 13, 2020. Accessed September 19, 2020. www. brookings.edu/blog/the-avenue/2020/02/13/discriminatory-housing-practices-are-leading-to-the-devaluation-of-black-americans/.

- Quigley, Bill. "14 Shocking Facts That Prove the US Criminal Justice System Is Racist." OpenDemocracy. 27 July 2010. Accessed September 19, 2020. www.opendemocracy.net/en/14-shocking-facts-that-prove-us-criminal-justice-system-is-racist/.

- "What Is Systemic Racism?" United States Conference of Catholic Bishops. n.d. Accessed September 20, 2020. www. usccb.org/issues-and-action/human-life-and-dignity/racism/upload/racism-and-systemic-racism.pdf.

- Young, Christen Linke. "There Are Clear, Race-Based Inequalities in Health Insurance and Health Outcomes." Brookings. February 20, 2020. Accessed September 19, 2020. www.brookings.edu/blog/usc-brookings-schaeffer-on-health-policy/2020/02/19/there-are-clear-race-based-inequalities-in-health-insurance-and-health-outcomes/.

Intermission: Shocking Racist Traditions

The African Dodger

- "The African Dodger." Ferris State University. 2012. Accessed September 19, 2020. www.ferris.edu/HTMLS/news/jimcrow/ question/2012/october.htm.

The Minstrel Show

- "Blackface: The Sad History of Minstrel Shows." American Heritage. 2019. Accessed September 24, 2020. www. americanheritage.com/blackface-sad-history-minstrel-shows.

Black Pete and Blackface

- Garen, Micah et al. "Zwarte Piet: Black Pete Is 'Dutch Racism in Full Display.' " Aljazeera. November 27, 2019. Accessed September 21, 2020. www.aljazeera.com/indepth/ features/zwarte-piet-black-pete-dutch-racism-full-display-181127153936872.html.

Gator Bait

- Foxworth, Domonique. "The Gut-Wrenching History of Black Babies and Alligators." The Undefeated. June 22, 2016. Accessed September 19, 2020. theundefeated.com/features/the-gut-wrenching-history-of-black-babies-and-alligators/.

- Henry, Carma. 2019. "Research Reveals That Black Children Were Fed to Hogs and Used as Alligator Bait in the Early 1900s." *The Westside Gazette.* July 6, 2019. Accessed September 24, 2020. thewestsidegazette.com/research-reveals-that-black-children-were-fed-to-hogs-and-used-as-alligator-bait-in-the-early-1900s/

- Strouse, Chuck. "Black Babies Used as Alligator Bait in Florida." *Miami New Times*. February 3, 2014. Accessed September 19, 2020. www.miaminewtimes.com/news/black-babies-used-as-alligator-bait-in-florida-6531453.

Blacks and Medical Malpractice

- "Fannie Lou Hamer." American Experience. PBS. 2000. Accessed September 24, 2020. www.pbs.org/wgbh/americanexperience/features/freedomsummer-hamer/.

- Gordon, Taylor. "5 Unethical Medical Experiments That Used Black People as Guinea Pigs." Atlanta Black Star. December 2, 2014. Accessed September 24, 2020. atlantablackstar.com/2014/12/02/5-unethical-medical-experiments-that-used-black-people-as-guinea-pigs/.

- Rothman, Lily. "The Disturbing History of African-Americans and Medical Research Goes Beyond Henrietta Lacks." *Time*. April 21, 2017. Accessed September 24, 2020. time.com/4746297/henrietta-lacks-movie-history-research-oprah/.

- "The Impact of Racism on Children's Health." Dayton Children's. June 4, 2020. Accessed September 24, 2020. www.childrensdayton.org/the-hub/impact-racism-childrens-health.

Racist Songs, Racist Commercials, Racist Objects

- Abad-Santos, Alex. "What Should We Do with Our Racist Folk Songs?" Vox. May 21, 2014. Accessed September 24, 2020. www.vox.com/2014/5/21/5732258/the-racist-childrens-songs-you-might-not-have-known-were-racist.

- Pilgrim, David. "Why I Collect Racist Objects." Jim Crow Museum | Ferris State University. n.d. Accessed September 20, 2020. www.ferris.edu/HTMLS/news/jimcrow/collect.htm.

Should we pretend the past didn't happen?

- Bishara, Hakim. 2020. "Toppled and Defaced Racist Monuments in 15 Cities, From Richmond to Bristol." Hyperallergic. June 10, 2020. Accessed September 19, 2020. hyperallergic.com/569756/confederate-monuments-removed/.

- Jacob, Mark. "10 Things You Might Not Know about Racism." *Chicago Tribune.* January 17, 2010. Accessed September 19, 2020. www.chicagotribune.com/chi-10-things-racism-story.html.

- McLaughlin, Eliott C. "Honoring the Unforgivable: The Horrific Acts behind the Names on America's Infamous Monuments and Tributes." CNN. June 17, 2020. Accessed September 19, 2020. www.cnn.com/2020/06/16/us/racist-statues-controversial-monuments-in-america-robert-lee-columbus/index.html.

- Morris, Phillip. "As Monuments Fall, How Does the World Reckon with a Racist Past?" National Geographic. June 30, 2020. Accessed September 19, 2020. www.nationalgeographic.co.uk/history-and-civilisation/2020/06/as-monuments-fall-how-does-the-world-reckon-with-a-racist-past

Chapter 8: Microaggressions

- "10 Things NEVER to Say to a Black Coworker." DiversityInc. July 17, 2009. Accessed September 19, 2020. www.diversityinc.com/10-things-never-to-say-to-a-black-coworker/.

• Abbensetts, Kwesi. "You're Pretty, for A Black Girl." Those People. n.d. Accessed September 20, 2020. www.thsppl.com/thsppl-articles/2017/4/27/youre-pretty-for-a-blackgirl.

• Akyianu, Simone Aba. "Touching Black Hair as Micro-Aggression." Parents for Diversity. August 25, 2019. Accessed September 19, 2020. www.parentsfordiversity.com/post/touching-black-hair-as-micro-aggression.

• Asare, Janice Gassam. "Why The 'I Don't See Color' Mantra Is Hurting Your Diversity and Inclusion Efforts." *Forbes*. February 15, 2019. Accessed September 20, 2020. www.forbes.com/sites/janicegassam/2019/02/15/why-the-i-dont-see-color-mantra-is-hurting-diversity-and-inclusion-efforts/#2b49bbf12c8d.

• Baker, Paxton K. "Why Saying 'All Lives Matter' Misses the Big Picture." CNN. June 23, 2020. Accessed September 19, 2020. www.cnn.com/2020/06/23/opinions/all-lives-matter-misses-the-big-picture-baker/index.html.

• Blay, Zeba. "For the Umpteenth Time: Having A Black 'Friend' Doesn't Mean You Aren't Racist." HuffPost. August 16, 2017. Accessed September 19, 2020. www.huffpost.com/entry/for-the-umpteenth-time-having-a-black-friend-doesnt-mean-you-arent-racist_n_59948617e4b0d0d2cc83a9af.

• Bond, Victoria. "It's Time to Abandon the 'acting White' Theory Once and for All." *The Guardian*. October 22, 2014. Accessed September 24, 2020. www.theguardian.com/commentisfree/2014/oct/22/acting-white-theory-dear-white-people-college.

• Capatides, Christina. "Why Saying 'All Lives Matter' Communicates to Black People That Their Lives Don't." CBS News. July 8, 2020. Accessed September 1, 2020. www.cbsnews.com/news/all-lives-matter-black-lives-matter/.

• Carroll, Rebecca. "I Thought I Was a Gorgeous Kid until I Learned I Was Just 'pretty, for a Black Girl.' " *The Guardian*.

February 4, 2016. Accessed September 19, 2020. www.
theguardian.com/commentisfree/2016/feb/04/i-thought-i-
was-a-gorgeous-kid-until-i-learned-i-was-just-pretty-for-a-
black-girl.

- Chaffers, Julia. "The Problem with Saying 'I Don't See Color.' "
  The Princetonian. February 20, 2019. September 19, 2020.
  www.dailyprincetonian.com/article/2019/02/the-problem-
  with-saying-i-dont-see-color.

- Crews, Kris. "Stop Telling Me I'm 'Pretty for A Black Girl.' "
  MTV News. April 8, 2016. Accessed September 20, 2020. www.
  mtv.com/news/2862057/stop-telling-me-im-pretty-for-a-
  black-girl/.

- DeAngelis, Tori. "Unmasking 'racial microaggressions.' "
  American Psychological Association. February 2009.
  Accessed September 1, 2020. www.apa.org/monitor/2009/02/
  microaggression.

- Dennis, Riley J. "You Can Have a Black Friend AND Be
  Racist." YouTube. December 18, 2016. Accessed September 19,
  2020. www.youtube.com/watch?v=3TBIb8soUEI.

- Desmond-Harris, Jenée. "The Myth about Smart Black
  Kids and 'Acting White' That Won't Die." Vox. January
  5, 2017. Accessed September 19, 2020. www.vox.com/
  identities/2017/1/5/14175116/acting-white-myth-black-kids-
  academics-school-achievement-gap-debunked.

- " 'Don't Touch My Hair:' These Black Men Are Pushing Back
  against Everyday Racism." CBS News. Feb 6, 2020. September
  19, 2020. www.youtube.com/watch?v=PADEoOY21JM.

- "Examples of Racial Microaggressions." University of
  Minnesota. n.d. Accessed September 19, 2020. sph.umn.edu/
  site/docs/hewg/microaggressions.pdf.

- Ferlazzo, Larry. "Saying 'I Don't See Color' Denies the Racial
  Identity of Students." Classroom Q&A with Larry Ferlazzo.

2020. Accessed September 19, 2020. blogs.edweek.org/teachers/
classroom_qa_with_larry_ferlazzo/2020/02/saying_i_dont_
see_color_denies_the_racial_identity_of_students.html.

- Fletcher, Kennedy. " 'You're Pretty for a Black Girl!' Stop the
  Hate Youth Speak Out Fourth-Place Winner." Cleveland. May
  15, 2020. Accessed September 24, 2020. www.cleveland.com/
  news/2020/05/youre-pretty-for-a-black-girl-stop-the-hate-
  youth-speak-out-finalist.html

- Hales, Ajah. "5 Phrases Your Black Friend Wishes You Would
  Stop Using." Medium. January 23, 2020. Accessed September
  19, 2020. zora.medium.com/5-phrases-your-black-friend-
  wishes-you-would-stop-using-c857cd415c5.

- Helligar, Jeremy. "When White People Say They Don't See
  Color." Medium. March 4, 2020. Accessed on September 19,
  2020. level.medium.com/when-white-people-say-they-dont-
  see-color-5b57a5bb933a.

- Hill, Jarrett. "Opinion: Dear Tomi Lahren, Please Stop Saying
  That You 'Don't See Color.' " NBC News. December 1, 2016.
  Accessed September 20, 2020. www.nbcnews.com/news/
  nbcblk/opinion-dear-tomi-lahren-please-stop-saying-you-
  dont-see-n690801

- Kelly, Ryan. "Explained: Why 'White Lives Matter' and 'All
  Lives Matter' Misses the Point of Black Lives Matter." Goal.
  com. June 24, 2020. Accessed September 19, 2020. www.goal.
  com/en-us/news/explained-why-white-lives-matter-all-lives-
  matter-misses/1wud91m963jo318648p0s2rwg8.

- Linly, Zack. "University of Michigan-Dearborn Apologizes
  for Hosting 'Non-POC Cafe' Event. Yep, You Read That
  Right." The Root. September 10, 2020. Accessed September
  20, 2020. www.theroot.com/university-of-michigan-dearborn-
  apologizes-for-hosting-1845012569.

- Louie, Sam. " 'I Don't See Color.' " *Psychology Today.* 2016. Accessed September 24, 2020. www.psychologytoday.com/us/ blog/minority-report/201602/i-dont-see-color.

- Marshall, Yannick. "(In)Articulate While Black." Black Perspectives. April 2, 2020. Accessed September 19, 2020. www.aaihs.org/inarticulate-while-black/.

- McCowan, Isami. "Why Black People Are Tired of Being Called 'Articulate.' " *Affinity Magazine.* December 29, 2016. Accessed September 19, 2020. affinitymagazine.us/2016/12/28/ why-black-people-are-tired-of-being-called-articulate/.

- McKenzie, Sam Jr. "I've Been Accused of 'Acting White,' but I'm Not the Real Problem." Medium. December 6, 2019. Accessed September 24, 2020. level.medium.com/theres-a-difference-between-acting-white-and-reacting-white-17627500c4d5.

- McWhorter, John. " 'Acting White' Remains a Barrier for Black Education." Reason.Com. October 8, 2014. Accessed September 24, 2020. reason.com/2014/10/08/acting-white-remains-a-barrier-for-black/.

- McWhorter, John. "No, 'Acting White' Has Not Been Debunked." The Daily Beast, September 4, 2014. Accessed September 19, 2020. www.thedailybeast.com/no-acting-white-has-not-been-debunked.

- McWhorter, John. "The Origins of the 'Acting White' Charge." *The Atlantic.* July 20, 2019. Accessed September 19, 2020. www.theatlantic.com/ideas/archive/2019/07/acting-white-charge-origins/594130/.

- Mukando, Tariro. "What It Really Means When You Ask, 'Can I Touch Your Hair?' " *Fashion Journal.* January 24, 2020. Accessed September 19, 2020. fashionjournal.com.au/beauty/ what-it-really-means-when-you-ask-can-i-touch-your-hair/.

- Norman, Jill et al. " 'You Must Have Voted for Obama': 5 Things NEVER to Say to Blacks." DiversityInc. February 18, 2013. Accessed September 24, 2020. www.diversityinc.com/ you-must-have-voted-for-obama-5-things-never-to-say-to-blacks/.

- Opiah, Antonia. "Can I Touch Your Hair?" HuffPost. May 28, 2013. Accessed September 19, 2020. www.huffpost.com/entry/ can-i-touch-your-hair_b_3320122.

- Osterheldt, Jenee. "Don't Touch Our Hair." Aperture Foundation NY. December 9, 2016. Accessed September 19, 2020. aperture.org/blog/dont-touch-our-hair/.

- Paul, Susan Joy. "I'm Not Racist, but…" *Colorado Springs Gazette*. June 23, 2020. Accessed September 19, 2020. gazette. com/woodmenedition/i-m-not-racist-but-northwest-notes/ article_680684a6-af34-11ea-88ab-c37670d461cd.html.

- Pavlovitz, John. "Of Course You See Color When Looking at People—or at Least You Should." Stuff That Needs To Be Said. June 6, 2016. Accessed September 19, 2020. johnpavlovitz. com/2016/06/06/of-course-you-see-color-or-at-least-you-should/.

- Rogers, Kristen. "Dear anti-racist allies: Here's how to respond to microaggressions." CNN. June 5, 2020. Accessed July 20, 2020. www.cnn.com/2020/06/05/health/racial-microaggressions-examples-responses-wellness/index.html.

- Russ, Valerie and Anna Orso. "How Saying 'I Don't See Color' Went from Woke to Whitewashing." *The Philadelphia Inquirer*. February 15, 2019. Accessed September 20, 2020. www.inquirer.com/news/howard-schultz-i-dont-see-race-colorblind-starbucks-philadelphia-arrests-20190215.html.

- "Saying 'All Lives Matter' Doesn't Make You Racist, Just Extremely Ignorant." Cleveland.com. June 29, 2020. Accessed September 19, 2020. www.cleveland.com/

entertainment/2020/06/saying-all-lives-matter-doesnt-make-you-racist-just-extremely-ignorant.html.

- Scruggs, Afi-Odelia E. "Colorblindness: The New Racism?" Teaching Tolerance. 2009. Accessed September 19, 2020. www.tolerance.org/magazine/fall-2009/colorblindness-the-new-racism.

- Shahvisi, Arianne. "The Philosophical Flaw in Saying 'All Lives Matter.' " *Prospect.* July 3, 2020. Accessed September 19, 2020. www.prospectmagazine.co.uk/philosophy/black-lives-matter-essay-why-is-saying-all-lives-matter-wrong.

- Shelton, David. "Let's Stop Pretending and Saying That We Don't See Color." *The Leaf-Chronicle.* June 9, 2020. Accessed September 20, 2020. www.theleafchronicle.com/story/opinion/columnists/2020/06/09/lets-stop-pretending-and-saying-we-dont-see-color-opinion/5326374002/.

- Staunton, John. "My Family Never Owned Any Slaves." Racismreview.com. June 13, 2008. Accessed September 19, 2020. theracecardproject.com/never-owned-slaves/.

- Stephens, Britt. "4 Things I've Learned from Being Pretty 'For a Black Girl.' " Popsugar. January 8, 2020. Accessed September 19, 2020. www.popsugar.com/love/Pretty-Black-Girl-37877996.

- Thomas, Brian C. "If You Say: 'I'm Not Racist, I Have an African-American Friend' Read This." Chicagonow.com. June 9, 2020. Accessed September 20, 2020. www.chicagonow.com/your-doubting-thomas/2020/06/if-you-say-im-not-racist-i-have-an-african-american-friend-read-this/.

- Tough, Paul. " 'Acting White' Myth, The." *The New York Times*, December 12, 2004. Accessed September 19, 2020. www.nytimes.com/2004/12/12/magazine/acting-white-myth-the.html.

- Tutu, Nana. " 'Pretty for a Black Girl' Isn't a Compliment." The Current. March 7, 2017. Accessed September 20, 2020. wmcurrent.com/7605/opinion/pretty-for-a-black-girl-isnt-a-compliment/.

- Vaughan, Darrah. "I'm Not Racist, But…" Moonshine Ink. June 12, 2020. Accessed September 19, 2020. www.moonshineink.com/opinion/im-not-racist-but/.

- Ward, Marguerite and Rachel Premack. "What Is a Microaggression? 14 Things People Think Are Fine to Say at Work—but Are Actually Racist, Sexist, or Offensive." Business Insider. July 24, 2020. Accessed September 19, 2020. www.businessinsider.com/microaggression-unconscious-bias-at-work-2018-6#oh-sorry-wrong-person-3.

- Whitfield, David. "Colorblindness Is a Form of Racism, a Nemesis, and a Barrier to Dismantling It." *The Olympian.* September 2, 2020. Accessed September 19, 2020. www.theolympian.com/opinion/op-ed/article227280259.html.

- Wingfield, Adia Harvey. "Why Color-Blindness Is a Counterproductive Ideology." *The Atlantic.* September 13, 2015. Accessed September 19, 2020. www.theatlantic.com/politics/archive/2015/09/color-blindness-is-counterproductive/405037/.

- Woods, S. "Wow! You're so Articulate!" The Race Card Project. May 13, 2014. Accessed September 19, 2020. theracecardproject.com/wow-youre-articulate/.

- Yeboah, Stephanie. "I Don't Care If You're 'fascinated' by My Afro, Stop Touching It." Metro. September 9, 2019. Accessed September 19, 2020. metro.co.uk/2019/09/09/i-dont-care-if-youre-fascinated-by-my-afro-stop-touching-it-10708877/.

Racist Expressions

- Helligar, Jeremy. "12 Everyday Expressions That Are Actually Racist." *Reader's Digest*. June 17, 2020. Accessed September 20, 2020. www.rd.com/list/everyday-expressions-that-are-racist/.

- Morris, Natalie. "What to Do If Your White Friends Keep Saying the Wrong Things about Racism." Metro. June 4, 2020. Accessed September 19, 2020. metro.co.uk/2020/06/04/how-talk-white-friends-keep-saying-wrong-things-about-racism-12805723/.

Reverse Racism

- Lewis, Philip. "Here's Why 'Reverse Racism' Doesn't Actually Exist in the US." Business Insider. April 15, 2016. Accessed September 19, 2020. www.businessinsider.com/heres-why-reverse-racism-doesnt-actually-exist-in-the-us-2016-4.

- Manisha Krishnan. "Dear White People, Please Stop Pretending Reverse Racism Is Real." *Vice*. October 2, 2016. Accessed September 19, 2020. www.vice.com/en_us/article/kwzjvz/dear-white-people-please-stop-pretending-reverse-racism-is-real.

- Newkirk II, Vann R. "Affirmative Action and the Myth of Reverse Racism." *The Atlantic*. August 5, 2017. Accessed September 19, 2020. www.theatlantic.com/education/archive/2017/08/myth-of-reverse-racism/535689/.

- "Reverse Racism." Alberta Civil Liberties Research Centre. n.d. Accessed September 19, 2020. www.aclrc.com/myth-of-reverse-racism.

Intersectionality

- Coaston, Jane. "Intersectionality, Explained: Meet Kimberlé Crenshaw, Who Coined the Term." Vox. May 20, 2019. Accessed September 19, 2020. www.vox.com/the-highlight/2019/5/20/18542843/intersectionality-conservatism-law-race-gender-discrimination.

- D'Cruz, Carolyn. "Explainer: What Does 'intersectionality' Mean?" The Conversation. February 26, 2019. Accessed September 19, 2020. theconversation.com/explainer-what-does-intersectionality-mean-104937.

- Kort, Joe. "Understanding Intersectional Identities." *Psychology Today*. June 25, 2019. Accessed September 19, 2020. www.psychologytoday.com/us/blog/understanding-the-erotic-code/201906/understanding-intersectional-identities.

- "What Is Intersectionality, and What Does It Have to Do with Me?" YW Boston. March 29, 2017. Accessed September 19, 2020 www.ywboston.org/2017/03/what-is-intersectionality-and-what-does-it-have-to-do-with-me/.

Chapter 9: Support Your Child's Creativity

- Carter, Christine. "7 Ways to Foster Creativity in Your Kids." Greater Good. September 16, 2008. Accessed September 19, 2020. greatergood.berkeley.edu/article/item/7_ways_to_foster_creativity_in_your_kids.

- Tartakovsky, Margarita. "9 Ways to Support Your Child's Creativity." World of Psychology. July 8, 2018. Accessed September 19, 2020. psychcentral.com/blog/9-ways-to-support-your-childs-creativity/.

How to Encourage Confidence

- "10 Tips on How to Build Confidence in Kids." Working Mother. June 7, 2019. Accessed September 20, 2020. www. workingmother.com/content/10-tips-helping-your-child-build-self-confidence#page-2.

- "12 Tips to Raise Confident Children." Child Mind Institute. n.d. Accessed September 20, 2020. childmind.org/article/12-tips-raising-confident-kids/.

- Cullins, Ashley. "25 Things You Can Do Right Now to Build a Child's Confidence." Big Life Journal. 2017. Accessed September 24, 2020. biglifejournal.com/blogs/blog/child-confidence.

- Howard, Jacqueline. "New Study Confirms Depressing Truth About Names and Racial Bias." HuffPost. October 8, 2015. Accessed on September 19, 2020. www.huffpost.com/entry/black-sounding-names-study_n_561697a5e4b0dbb8000d687f.

- Markham, Laura. "12 Ways to Raise a Competent, Confident Child with Grit." *Psychology Today.* June 5, 2015. Accessed September 19, 2020. www.psychologytoday.com/us/blog/peaceful-parents-happy-kids/201506/12-ways-raise-competent-confident-child-grit.

- Millner, Denene. "Black Boys and Self-Esteem: How to Silence Your Son's Inner Critic." MyBrownBaby. April 28, 2014. Accessed on September 19, 2020. mybrownbaby.com/2014/04/black-boys-and-self-esteem-how-to-silence-your-sons-inner-critic/.

- Morin, Amanda. "7 Ways to Help Your Child Develop Positive Self-Esteem." Understood.org. August 5, 2019. Access September 19, 2020. www.understood.org/en/friends-feelings/empowering-your-child/self-esteem/7-ways-to-boost-your-childs-self-esteem.

- Morton, Victoria. "Boosting Self-Esteem in African American Children Starts with Family and Heritage." Scripps Howard Foundation Wire. December 10, 2002. Accessed September 19, 2020. www.shfwire.com/boosting-self-esteem-african-american-children-starts-family-and-heritage/.

- Ruekberg, Benjamin. "Building Self-Esteem in African American Males." The College at Brockport: State University of New York. 2006. Accessed September 20, 2020. digitalcommons.brockport.edu/cgi/viewcontent.cgi?article=1091&context=edc_theses

- "Self Esteem in Children of Color." Adoptive Families Association of BC. August 5, 2013. Accessed September 19, 2020. www.bcadoption.com/resources/articles/self-esteem-children-color.

- Smith, Jacquelyn. "A Psychologist Says Parents Should Do These 18 Things to Raise a More Confident Child." Business Insider. November 9, 2016. Accessed September 19, 2020. www.businessinsider.com/psychologist-explains-how-to-raise-a-more-confident-child-2016-11.

Chapter 10: Self-Advocacy

- "10 Steps to Being an Effective Self-Advocate." Mental Health Recovery. n.d. Accessed September 19, 2020. mentalhealthrecovery.com/info-center/ten-steps-to-being-an-effective-self-advocate/.

- "10 Steps to Effective Self-Advocacy." Disability Rights Florida. n.d. Accessed September 20, 2020. disabilityrightsflorida.org/resources/disability_topic_info/10_steps_to_effective_self_advocacy.

- "Be Your Own Best Advocate." Pacer.org. n.d. Accessed September 19, 2020. www.pacer.org/parent/php/PHP-c116.pdf.

- "How You Can Help Your Child Learn to Be a Good Self-Advocate." Pacer.org. n.d. Accessed September 19, 2020. www.pacer.org/parent/php/PHP-c95.pdf.

- "How to Self-Advocate". Mental Health Recovery. n.d. Accessed September 20, 2020. mentalhealthrecovery.com/info-center/how-to-self-advocate/.

- Lee, Andrew M.I. "The Importance of Self-Advocacy for Kids Who Learn and Think Differently." Understood.org. n.d. Accessed on September 19, 2020. www.understood.org/en/friends-feelings/empowering-your-child/self-advocacy/the-importance-of-self-advocacy.

- Morin, Amanda. "6 Tips for Helping Your High-Schooler Learn to Self-Advocate." Understood.com. n.d. Accessed September 19, 2020. www.understood.org/en/friends-feelings/empowering-your-child/self-advocacy/6-tips-for-helping-your-high-schooler-learn-to-self-advocate.

Racism in the Schools

- Antoninis, Manos. "We Need to Talk about Racism in Schools." *The Hill.* June 29, 2020. Accessed September 20, 2020. thehill.com/opinion/education/505113-we-need-to-talk-about-racism-in-schools.

- Farmer, George. "What Racism in Schools Looks Like." *Education Next.* June 23, 2020. Accessed on September 19, 2020. www.educationnext.org/what-racism-in-schools-looks-like-how-to-start-fixing-it/

- Furfaro, Hannah. "To Understand Structural Racism, Look to Our Schools." *The Seattle Times.* June 28, 2020. Accessed September 19, 2020. www.seattletimes.com/education-lab/to-understand-structural-racism-look-to-our-schools/.

- Howard, Tyrone C. "How to Root Out Anti-Black Racism from Your School." *Education Week.* June 10, 2020. Accessed

September 19, 2020. www.edweek.org/ew/articles/2020/06/04/
how-to-root-out-anti-black-racism-from.html.

- McKamey, Pirette. "What Anti-Racist Teachers Do
  Differently." *The Atlantic.* June 17, 2020. Accessed September
  19, 2020. www.theatlantic.com/education/archive/2020/06/
  how-be-anti-racist-teacher/613138/.

- Newman, Portia. "Causes and Effects of Racism in Schools."
  Kickboard. September 20, 2019. Accessed September 20, 2020.
  www.kickboardforschools.com/blog/post/diversity-equity/
  causes-and-effects-of-racism-in-schools/.

- Nittle, Nadra Kareem. "How Racism Affects Minority Students
  in Public Schools." ThoughtCo. February 25, 2020. Accessed
  September 20, 2020. www.thoughtco.com/how-racism-affects-
  public-school-minorities-4025361.

- "The Condition of Education." National Center for Education
  Statistics. May 2020. Accessed September 24, 2020. nces.
  ed.gov/programs/coe/indicator_coi.asp

Health Impact of Racism

- Assari, Shervin, Ehsan Moazen-Zadeh, Cleopatra Howard
  Caldwell, and Marc A. Zimmerman. "Racial Discrimination
  during Adolescence Predicts Mental Health Deterioration in
  Adulthood: Gender Differences among Blacks." *Frontiers in
  Public Health*, 29 May 2017. Accessed September 19, 2020. doi.
  org/10.3389/fpubh.2017.00104.

- Panko, Ben. 2017. "Racism Harms Children's Health, Survey
  Finds." Smithsonian.com. May 5, 2017. Accessed September
  19, 2020. www.smithsonianmag.com/science-nature/racism-
  harms-childrens-health-180963167/.

The Mental Toll of Racism

- Bonvillian, Crystal. "School's Failure to Stop Racist, Sexist Bullying Led to 9-Year-Old Girl's Suicide, Lawsuit States." WFXT. October 14, 2019. Accessed September 19, 2020. www. boston25news.com/news/trending/schools-failure-stop-racist-sexist-bullying-led-9-year-old-girls-suicide-lawsuit-states/ X7EZ7YL6TVGG3H2WBCF3HEL2PE/.

- Christensen, Jen. "Crisis Text Line Offers Help to Those in Need, One Text at a Time." CNN. October 14, 2019. Accessed September 19, 2020. www.cnn.com/2019/10/14/health/black-teen-suicide-attempts-study/index.html.

- Faulkner, Alison. "The Impact of Racism on Mental Health." National Elf Service. April 12, 2019. Accessed September 19, 2020. www.nationalelfservice.net/populations-and-settings/ black-and-minority-ethnic/racism-mental-health/.

- Ferdinand, Angeline S, Yin Paradies, and Margaret Kelaher. "Mental Health Impacts of Racial Discrimination in Australian Culturally and Linguistically Diverse Communities: A Cross-Sectional Survey." BMC Public Health. April 18, 2015. Accessed September 19, 2020. doi.org/10.1186/s12889-015-1661-1.

- Hanning, Judy. "Stress and Early Brain Growth (Infograph)." Learning Success. August 31, 2017. Accessed September 19, 2020. www.learningsuccessblog.com/stress-and-early-brain-growth-infograph-0.

- "How Racism Affects Youth Health and Well-Being." *Psychology Today*. 27 August 2019. Accessed September 19, 2020. www.psychologytoday.com/us/blog/evidence-based-living/201908/how-racism-affects-youth-health-and-well-being.

- Lindsey, Michael A., Arielle H. Sheftall, Yunyu Xiao, and Sean Joe. "Trends of Suicidal Behaviors Among High School

Students in the United States: 1991–2017." *Pediatrics.* November 2019. Accessed September 19, 2020. doi. org/10.1542/peds.2019-1187.

- Moore, Darnell L. "Why We Need to Talk About Racism as a Mental-Health Trigger." Mic. June 1, 2016. Accessed September 20, 2020. www.mic.com/articles/142534/ why-we-need-to-talk-about-racism-as-a-mental-health-trigger#.0x7lDCuDC.

- Moreland-Capuia, Alisha. "The Psychological Impact of Racism." American College of Physicians. November 6, 2018. Accessed September 19, 2020. www.acponline.org/system/ files/documents/about_acp/chapters/or/acpmtg-2018talk-moreland-alisha-psychologicalimpactofracism.pdf.

- Morris, Natalie. "The Damaging Psychological Impact of Constantly Having to Explain Racism." Metro. February 25, 2020. Accessed September 19, 2020. metro.co.uk/2020/02/25/ psychological-impact-constantly-explain-racism-12147969/.

- Runcie, Ayanna. "Suicide Attempts Increasing among Black Children and Teens, Study Finds." Cbsnews.com. October 14, 2019. Accessed September 19, 2020. www.cbsnews.com/news/ suicide-attempts-increasing-among-black-children-and-teens/.

- Samuel, Isoke and James Wellemeyer. "Black Students Experience Trauma from Racist Incidents at School, Experts Say." NBC News. July 4, 2020. Accessed September 19, 2020. www.nbcnews.com/news/nbcblk/black-students-experience-trauma-racist-incidents-school-experts-say-n1232829.

- Walker, Rheeda. "Black Kids and Suicide: Why Are Rates So High, and so Ignored?" The Conversation. January 17, 2020. Accessed September 19, 2020. theconversation.com/black-kids-and-suicide-why-are-rates-so-high-and-so-ignored-127066.

- Wortham, Jenna. "Racism's Psychological Toll," *The New York Times.* June 24, 2015. Accessed September 24,

2020. www.nytimes.com/2015/06/24/magazine/racisms-psychological-toll.html.

Coping Strategies | Bridging the Racial Divide

- "10 Steps Toward Bridging Our Painful Racial Divide." Not in Our Town. May 16, 2012. Accessed September 19, 2020. www.niot.org/blog/ywca-10-steps-toward-bridging-our-painful-racial-divide.

- "Beyond the Golden Rule: A Teaching Tolerance Publication." Tolerance.org. n.d. Accessed September 24, 2020. www.tolerance.org/sites/default/files/general/beyond_golden_rule.pdf.

- Gold, Mark. "The Impact of Racism and Mindfulness on Health." Addiction Policy Forum. June 20, 2019. Accessed September 19, 2020. www.addictionpolicy.org/post/the-impact-of-racism-and-mindfulness-on-health.

- Graham-LoPresti, Jessica R. "How Black Americans Can Cope with Anxiety and Racism." Anxiety.org. March 16, 2017. Accessed September 19, 2020. www.anxiety.org/black-americans-how-to-cope-with-anxiety-and-racism.

- Macedo, D. M., L. G. Smithers, R. M. Roberts, Y. Paradies, and L. M. Jamieson. 2019. "Effects of Racism on the Socio-Emotional Wellbeing of Aboriginal Australian Children." *International Journal for Equity in Health.* August 22, 2019. Accessed September 19, 2020. doi.org/10.1186/s12939-019-1036-9.

- Parker, Louisa Adjoa. "Building Resilience in a Racist World." Wellcome Collection. March 17, 2020. Accessed September 19, 2020. wellcomecollection.org/articles/XmipCBIAACAAfBOd.

- Powell, Sana I. "Racism, Stress & Chronic Illness." The Curly Therapist. June 12, 2020. Accessed September 19, 2020. curlytherapist.com/2020/06/12/racism-stress-chronic-illness/.

Chapter 11: How to Help Make Your Community Safer

- "15 Ways You Can Make Your Community Safer." Barnes & Associates Sotheby's International Realty. December 11, 2019. Accessed September 19, 2020. www.basothebysrealty. com/2019/12/11/15-ways-you-can-make-your-community-safer/.

- Badger, Emily. "The Neighborhood Is Mostly Black. The Home Buyers Are Mostly White." *The New York Times.* April 27, 2019. Accessed September 19, 2020. www.nytimes. com/interactive/2019/04/27/upshot/diversity-housing-maps-raleigh-gentrification.html.

- Chacon, Ana. "Black Boys More Fearful in Whiter Neighborhoods, Study Finds." ABC News. August 14, 2018. Accessed September 20, 2020. abcnews.go.com/Health/ black-boys-fearful-whiter-neighborhoods-study-finds/ story?id=57156060.

- Chang, Alvin. "White America Is Quietly Self-Segregating." Vox. January 18, 2017. Accessed September 19, 2020. www. vox.com/2017/1/18/14296126/white-segregated-suburb-neighborhood-cartoon.

- "Framework for Safe Neighborhood and Innovative Partnerships." Boston.gov. 2017. Accessed September 20, 2020. www.boston.gov/sites/default/files/document-file-07-2018/2017-violence-prevention-plan.pdf.

- Love, Hanna and Jennifer S. Vey. "To Build Safe Streets, We Need to Address Racism in Urban Design." Brookings. August 28, 2019. Accessed September 19, 2020. www.brookings.edu/ blog/the-avenue/2019/08/28/to-build-safe-streets-we-need-to-address-racism-in-urban-design/.

- "Making Children, Families, and Communities Safer from Violence." Lapdonline.org. n.d. Accessed September 19,

2020. www.lapdonline.org/crime_prevention/content_basic_view/8807.

- McMahan, Dana. "I Wanted to Make My Community Safer and More Neighborly. The Advice I Got Surprised Me." NBC News. 17 August 2019. Accessed September 20, 2020. www.nbcnews.com/better/lifestyle/i-wanted-make-my-community-safer-more-neighborly-advice-i-ncna1037396.

- Robinson, Raz. "Black Parents Avoid America's White Suburbs to Keep Their Kids Safe." Fatherly.com. June 23, 2020. Accessed September 19, 2020. www.fatherly.com/love-money/black-parents-race-suburbs-childrens-safety/.

- "Ten Ways to Immediately Improve Your Neighborhood." Pueblo.us. n.d. Accessed September 20, 2020. www.pueblo.us/1391/Ten-Ways-to-Immediately-Improve-Your-Nei.

Chapter 12: When You're a Non-Black Parent to Your Black Child

- Borresen, Kelsey. "6 Things White Kids Say About Race That Parents Should Call Out Now." HuffPost. July 17, 2020. Accessed September 19, 2020. www.huffpost.com/entry/things-white-kids-say-race_l_5f0e00fdc5b63b8fc10f7f9b.

- Coolman, Holly Taylor. "White Parents Adopting Black Kids Raises Hard Questions. We Can All Learn from Them." *America Magazine.* July 8, 2020. Accessed September 19, 2020. www.americamagazine.org/politics-society/2020/07/08/white-parents-Black-kids-transracial-adoption.

- Hall, Beth. "Raising a Child of Color in America—While White." HoltInternational.org. n.d. Accessed September 19, 2020. holtinternational.org/adoption/parent-training/wp-content/uploads/2018/08/Raising-a-Child-of-Color-in-America-While-White-by-Beth-Hall.pdf.

- Holohan, Meghan. "White Parents, Black Kids: Group Helps Parents Bridge Cultural Gaps." January 12, 2017. Today.com. Accessed September 20, 2020. www.today.com/parents/white-parents-black-kids-group-helps-bridge-cultural-gaps-t124023.

- Sha, La. "What White Parents Should Know About Adopting Black Children." HuffPost. January 12, 2016. Accessed September 19, 2020. www.huffpost.com/entry/what-white-parents-adopting-black-children_b_8951402.

- "Talking to Kids about Race." Family. June 1, 2020. Accessed September 19, 2020. www.nationalgeographic.com/family/in-the-news/talking-about-race/#close.

- Tucker, Angela. "What Happens When White Parents Adopt Black Children and Move to Black Neighborhoods." *Yes! Magazine.* February 14, 2018. Accessed September 20, 2020. www.yesmagazine.org/social-justice/2018/02/14/what-happens-when-white-parents-adopt-black-children-and-move-to-black-neighborhoods.

- Valby, Karen. "The Realities of Raising a Kid of a Different Race." *Time.* n.d. Accessed September 19, 2020. time.com/the-realities-of-raising-a-kid-of-a-different-race.

- "What We Learned from Our Children: Raising Black Children Across Racial Lines Roundtable." The Cradle. June 6, 2018. Accessed September 19, 2020. www.cradle.org/blog/what-we-learned-our-children-raising-black-children-across-racial-lines-roundtable.

About the Author

Born in Port-au-Prince, Haiti, **M.J. Fievre** moved to the United States in 2002. She currently writes from Miami.

M.J.'s publishing career began as a teenager in Haiti. At nineteen years old, she signed her first book contract with Hachette-Deschamps in Haiti for the publication of a young adult book titled *La Statuette Maléfique*. Since then, M.J. has authored nine books in French that are widely read in Europe and the French Antilles. In 2013, One Moore Book released M.J.'s first children's book, *I Am Riding*, written in three languages: English, French, and Haitian Creole. In 2015, Beating Windward Press published M.J.'s memoir, *A Sky the Color of Chaos*, about her childhood in Haiti during the brutal regime of Jean-Bertrand Aristide.

M.J. Fievre is the author of *Happy, Okay? Poems about Anxiety, Depression, Hope, and Survival* (Books & Books Press, 2019) and *Badass Black Girl: Questions, Quotes, and Affirmations for Teens* (Mango Publishing, 2020). She helps others write their way through trauma, build community, and create social change. She works with veterans, disenfranchised youth, cancer patients and survivors, victims of domestic and sexual violence, minorities, the elderly, those with chronic illness or going through transitions, and any underserved population in need of writing as a form of therapy—even if they don't realize that they need writing or therapy.

A long-time educator and frequent keynote speaker (Tufts University, Massachusetts; Howard University, Washington, DC; the University of Miami, Florida; and Michael College, Vermont; and a panelist at the Association of Writers & Writing Programs Conference, AWP), M.J. is available for book club meetings, podcast presentations, interviews, and other author events.

Contact MJ @ 954-391-3398 or emailhappyokay@gmail.com.

Mango Publishing, established in 2014, publishes an eclectic list of books by diverse authors—both new and established voices— on topics ranging from business, personal growth, women's empowerment, LGBTQ studies, health, and spirituality to history, popular culture, time management, decluttering, lifestyle, mental wellness, aging, and sustainable living. We were recently named 2019 *and* 2020's #1 fastest growing independent publisher by *Publishers Weekly*. Our success is driven by our main goal, which is to publish high quality books that will entertain readers as well as make a positive difference in their lives.

Our readers are our most important resource; we value your input, suggestions, and ideas. We'd love to hear from you—after all, we are publishing books for you!

Please stay in touch with us and follow us at:

Facebook: Mango Publishing
Twitter: @MangoPublishing
Instagram: @MangoPublishing
LinkedIn: Mango Publishing
Pinterest: Mango Publishing

Newsletter: mangopublishinggroup.com/newsletter

Join us on Mango's journey to reinvent publishing, one book at a time.